ADOPT-A-BOOK
CHRISTMAS 2020

In loving memory of
James Murray Marchen

KE-UNION LE
LED 6 MONTHS

TORONTO,

he men deserve
he says.

that Local 183
ate contract with
orating different
rking conditions,
air to the other
s, who are bou
signed with

no ind
cials.
jo

on construct
McGuire, who last week
ys in solid bargaining
ties, with no sign of a

us demands

day both sides came
g with Maguire in a
k than ever. John
ess manager of Local
rers' union, told re-
ompany's demands
idiculous'' and asked
prepare a case for
Nally before the
Board with failure

union leader sent
tro chairman, the
rovincial cabinet,
utside party to step
"It seems our dif-
n't be solved by
nini said,
sse is the tunnel-
at S. McNally
o sign the same
subway contract-
July, raising base
an hour to $5.55.
the agreement
industry expires
the tunnel dis-
hen, S. McNally
tracts be-

been on a f
the partie si
ly has moved.'

rers' union has
picket lines arou
ing they are not on
out. The company
entrances after a
ut on the night of
he shift boss and a
over working hours
requirements.

al dispute

pute dragged on, the
it Commission began
looking for ways to bring pressure
on one of the parties to reach a
settlement or even to break the job
contract and get the work done by
another company.

"But this is a legal labor dispute
and therefore, under the terms o
our contract with McNally, the com
pany has to be given extra time,
says D. A. Elliott, the TTC's lawye
Frustrated by the legal angles, th

Toronto Daily Star

MONE

STOCK MARKET QUOTATIONS

running this stri

e Johnnie, he's

MORE THAN WE BARGAINED FOR

MORE THAN WE BARGAINED FOR

AN UNTOLD STORY *of*
EXPLOITATION, REDEMPTION,
and THE MEN WHO BUILT A
WORKER'S EMPIRE

JOHN STEFANINI

SUTHERLAND HOUSE

TORONTO, 2019

Sutherland House
416 Moore Ave., Suite 205
Toronto, ON M4G 1O9

Copyright © 2019 by John Stefanini

All rights reserved, including the right to reproduce this book or
portions thereof in any form whatsoever. For information on rights and
permissions or to request a special discount for bulk purchases, please
contact Sutherland House at info@sutherlandhousebooks.com

Sutherland House and logo are registered
trademarks of The Sutherland House Inc.

First hardcover edition, September 2019

If you are interested in inviting one of our authors to a live event or
media appearance, please contact publicity@sutherlandhousebooks.com
and visit our website at sutherlandhousebooks.com for more
information about our authors and their schedules.

Manufactured in Canada
Cover designed by Lena Yang
Cover photograph courtesy of Kenneth Whyte
Book composed by Karl Hunt

Library and Archives Canada Cataloguing in Publication
Title: More than we bargained for : an untold story of exploitation,
redemption, and the men who built a worker's empire / John Stefanini.
Names: Stefanini, Giancarlo, 1940- author.
Identifiers: Canadiana 20190082178 | ISBN 9781999439538 (hardcover)
Subjects: LCSH: Stefanini, Giancarlo, 1940- | LCSH: Labor leaders—Canada—
Biography. | LCSH: Laborers' International Union of North America.
Local 183—Officials and employees—Biography. | LCSH: Labor unions—
Canada—History—20th century. | CSH: Italian Canadians—
Biography. | LCGFT: Autobiographies.
Classification: LCC HD6525.S74 A3 2019 | DDC 331.88092—dc23

ISBN 978-1-9994395-3-8

DEDICATION

This book is for the multitude of hard-working immigrants who came to Canada from their devastated countries after the Second World War.

They received no government assistance, paid for their own doctors and medical care, and bought their own homes. While many were exploited and discriminated against, they were still grateful to Canada and to Canadians for giving them a second chance in life. They had limited education and could not speak either of Canada's official languages, yet with their sweat, sacrifices, and know-how they built great cities and started untold numbers of manufacturing businesses and commercial enterprises. They enriched this country culturally and economically and created the prosperity necessary to establish the great social benefits we all take for granted today.

I wrote this book to tell the story of how this generation of immigrants built the foundations of the construction-business labour unions in Toronto, and to describe the enormous impact our movement has had on Canada and its economy.

TABLE OF CONTENTS

CHAPTER 1 Nothing Left for Me in Italy   1

CHAPTER 2 The Sand Hog Tragedy   9

CHAPTER 3 The Strike of 1960   16

CHAPTER 4 My Start with Local 183   24

CHAPTER 5 Arrested on the Job   28

CHAPTER 6 An Altar Boy in Prison   38

CHAPTER 7 Street Cred   43

CHAPTER 8 The Expansion of Local 183   48

CHAPTER 9 The Safety Crusade   56

CHAPTER 10 The Strike of 1967   61

CHAPTER 11 Ethnic Conflicts and a Shotgun Meeting   64

CHAPTER 12 A Case of Indigestion   69

CHAPTER 13 Sudbury Saturday Night   78

CHAPTER 14 A Prophecy Come True   84

CHAPTER 15 The Right Stuff   95

CHAPTER 16 The Invisible Paycheque   100

CHAPTER 17 At War with Washington   108

CHAPTER 18 Firing a Union Steward   114

CHAPTER 19 A Dirty Business   120

CHAPTER 20 Local 183 in Adolescence   130

CHAPTER 21 "That Son of a Bitch!"   140

CHAPTER 22 Lessons in Negotiation   147

CHAPTER 23 Snapped at by Trudeau   154

CHAPTER 24 My Establishment Years   159

CHAPTER 25 You Can Go Home Again   168

CHAPTER 26 The Guardian Angels   176

CHAPTER 27 The Bombshell Agreement   186

CHAPTER 28 Changing of the Guard   192

CHAPTER 29 My Career as a Developer   197

CHAPTER 30 My Last Strike   215

CHAPTER 31 Lunch with the Police   220

CHAPTER 32 The New Ontario Government, 1990   225

CHAPTER 33 The Peace Treaties   230

CHAPTER 34 The Rescue of the Bricklayers   237

CHAPTER 35 The Labrador Tragedy   240

CHAPTER 36 My Departure   244

CHAPTER 37 On Negotiation   251

                Acknowledgements   259

CHAPTER 1

NOTHING LEFT FOR ME IN ITALY

When I immigrated to Canada in 1959, it was not without assistance. I was fortunate to have family already in Toronto. Thanks to my brother, Sergio, and my sister, Franca, my family sponsors, I was granted a visa. Sergio had been in Toronto for ten years and had prospered as a modest builder of homes. Franca arrived a few years before me and had a job at a bank.

I was born in 1940 in Polcenigo, in the province of Pordenone, part of the Friuli-Venezia Giulia region of Italy. My mother, Anna, was widowed at twenty-one. With no money and a lien on her property, she had to leave my older brother, Sergio, in Polcenigo to work as a domestic in Como. She later moved to Rome where she met my father. My sister, Franca, and I were born and for a time we lived in Rome where my father ran a restaurant. Unfortunately, the restaurant went broke and we moved back to Friuli just before I decided to come to Canada.

Rome is very much my home, as much as Polcenigo, but I was driven to Toronto at age eighteen by the success stories of

Sergio and Franca. I saw North America as the veritable prom-ised land. With their stories in my head, I applied for a visa at the first opportunity and when I got the instructions to report for a medical checkup at the Canadian Embassy in Rome I was on cloud nine. Truth be told, Canada was just a fuzzy place on the map for me, as it was for most Italians. In our minds, it was simply a part of North America and easily confused with the United States. We all know the difference now but Canada was a young country back then with a just-emerging identity forged in two world wars in which it had fought on behalf of the British Empire.

After my checkup, I went north to the small city of Sacile, which is the main station for the American air base in Aviano, in Pordenone province, known as the Garden of Serenissima, or the Republic of Venice, to say goodbye to my mother. I was buzzing with excitement when I got on that train to begin the longest journey of my life, a grand adventure of which I had dreamed for a long time.

I rode the train west to Genova, Christopher Columbus's birthplace, and boarded the SS *Irpinia*, a transatlantic ship built in 1929. It had seen better days. Operated by the famed Grimaldi family, it specialized in carrying immigrants to their new homes, which in my case was Montreal, one of the main ports of entry for passenger ships back then.

I was lucky because the SS *Irpinia* was small enough to slip up the St. Lawrence River. Bigger transatlantic liners carrying immi-grants could not do so. They had to dock in Halifax. Passengers in Halifax were then transferred onto trains specially fitted with uncomfortable wooden seats for the forty-eight-hour journey to Toronto. I heard many stories from Italians and other immigrants of that exhausting trip, first battling seasickness and then the jar-ring train ride.

For those arriving in Canada in winter, it was a real shock. Not only was the sea rougher in the winter but then they had to break the ice forming on the windowpanes just to see out of the train, and even then there were days when they saw nothing but snow. It was a far cry from sunny Italy. Little wonder these trains were dubbed *carri bestiami*, or cattle wagons. The traveling conditions were awful. Often there were not enough seats for the immigrants on the train. Their food was bought at the port grocery store before boarding. It consisted mainly of white sliced bread, nothing like the good homemade Italian bread to which they were accustomed.

But I was entering the country at Montreal, and after a ten-day crossing, the SS *Irpinia* arrived on a beautiful August day in 1959. I could not have been happier. I felt like celebrating. Thirsty for a cold beer, I bought one with the few dollars in my pocket, not thinking for a minute that you might have to be a certain age (twenty-one) to drink alcohol. I was eighteen and I got away with it. Of course, in Europe we start drinking legally at a much younger age.

Montreal seemed vaguely familiar as I explored it. I visited its Cathédral Marie-Reine-du-Monde and I noted to myself that it looked similar to Saint Peter's Basilica in Rome. As I admired it, I stopped to chat with a priest and in quite fair Italian he confirmed my impression. It was a quarter-scale replica of the Basilica, which, of course, I had visited often. In the afternoon I took the train to Toronto. Unlike those trains from Nova Scotia, its carriages had comfortable seats and air conditioning and it was a lovely journey. I arrived in Toronto at around 9:30 p.m. and hurried out of the station hoping to meet my family.

No one came to greet me so I grabbed a taxi and in rather poor English gave the driver the address of my uncle's home on Perth Avenue in west Toronto where my brother and sister, Sergio and Franca, lived. My attempt at English must have been impressive because the taxi driver got into a conversation with me, convinced I was fluent. I played along, limiting my responses to a "yes" from time to time.

At my uncle's home I found the door open but nobody inside. I learned later that in those days no one locked their doors because crime was almost non-existent in Toronto. Folks actually left money outside their doors to pay the milkman or the baker, who would make home deliveries. I knew I was in the right place when I saw on the piano a photograph of my cousin who at that time was on vacation with her mother in Italy. There was nothing to do but sit and wait so I made myself comfortable on the sofa, turned on the black-and-white TV, and watched an old movie.

An hour or so later the telephone rang. I answered it. It was my sister, Franca, and she obviously thought she was talking to my brother, Sergio.

"Sergio," she said in a very agitated voice. "We did not find Giancarlo. They all got off the train except him."

She was so worried and upset it took me quite a while to convince her that it was in fact me on the phone and that I was sitting on the sofa waiting for her at the house. Once she calmed down, she told me that since it was a hot night, they had gone to get ice cream while they were waiting for me. However, my train had arrived ahead of schedule and they weren't yet back at the station when it came in. I was the first one off the train and, not seeing them, I had jumped into a taxi.

It all ended well and I started adjusting to my new life in Canada. I learned that there were many other Italians, and more arriving every day, especially to Toronto. They came because there was very little left at home. Italy, like many other European countries, had been devastated by the war. Industries were shattered, there were no jobs, and millions of young Italians were forced to emigrate. Most were from the countryside, uneducated but with a strong work ethic and a will to overcome obstacles. We emigrated to the four corners of the earth: Australia, South America, North America, as well as France, Switzerland, and Belgium.

I was a lucky man. I came to Canada because I wanted to, not because I had no choice. Almost a million of us came to Canada over a twenty-year period. At the time the immigration branch at the Canadian Embassy in Italy was staffed with former army officers who had fought in Italy and come to know the people. To them, formal education was not as important as work ethic.

At first, it was very hard for these young Italian immigrants. The first and most important thing for them on arriving in Toronto was to find a job. Any job. In those days, on meeting people, the first question was, "Are you working?" Even before, "How are you?" A job was more important than health. We had no word for "welfare" and even if one had been available, our pride and desire to make a success would not have let us utter it, much less apply for it.

With Toronto starting to grow rapidly, many of us found jobs in construction and factories. We were mostly single and those who were married had left their spouses back home in order to build an economic base before bringing them over. A lot of the men slept four to eight in a room in houses owned by earlier Italian immigrants. They were called *bordanti*, adapted from the English "room and board." The lady of the house had to cook for them; do the laundry; and prepare their breakfast, lunches to take on the job, and dinner—in addition to looking after her own family. Such sacrifices were necessary to help the family pay the mortgage.

Slowly the immigrants were joined by their spouses and children or soon-to-be brides. The first dream of young couples was to buy a house, a dream that required untold sacrifices. Everyone worked. Wives worked in factories or as cleaning ladies. They got up early in the morning when it was still dark to take their children to other ladies who for a fee would look after them. Then they went to work for long hours. They returned home in the dark, picked up the children, and went home to do other household chores or prepare for the next day. Their husbands were also working long hours, returning home sometimes when their children were already asleep. I remember one worker telling me that he saw his children only on Sundays. In those days, we did not have weekends. Saturday was just another working day.

The construction industry was not as advanced as it is today and it was seasonal because of the weather. Jobs were scarce and the manpower was plentiful. Wages were low and cheating workers out of their pay was common. Paycheques came every two weeks, on a Friday, but quite often they bounced for insufficient funds and the bank usually took more than a week to communicate this news to the depositor. The upshot for many immigrant workers was that they had put in a month of brutal hours for nothing.

It was all ad hoc. Workers were picked up from assembly points and taken to the construction site in pickup trucks, each one half-covered by a cabin constructed of plywood. The other half of the truck bed was loaded with tools, picks, shovels, and wheelbarrows. It was not only unsafe but very uncomfortable especially during the winter. Workers ate their lunches at the site, in the open, regardless of the weather, or in shacks full of tools and unpleasant odours.

Safety on the job was at a minimum with no helmets, no safety shoes, weak scaffolding, and poor shoring in sewer trenches and other excavations. There was no regard for human life and immigrants like us were clearly seen as expendable. On-the-job accidents were frequent, and often fatal. The prevailing view of immigrants extended beyond the construction sites in Toronto, as we soon discovered. On Sundays we used to walk on College Street or St. Clair Avenue but if three or more of us gathered on the sidewalk, we were quickly dispersed by the police on the grounds that we were an "illegal assembly." To Toronto's largely white, Anglo-Saxon establishment, Italians were still seen as "the former enemy." Racism was rampant. We were called all kind of derogatory names: DPs (displaced persons), wops, dagos.

Life and health were fragile. Many prayed for good health because an illness could destroy their meagre savings. In those days, there was no medicare. We had to pay for our own doctors, hospitals, X-rays, and treatment. In some cases, the sick or injured had to resort to the support of relatives or friends.

Working conditions were bad enough that many immigrants would have returned to Italy if they had been able to afford the ticket, although the traumatic experience of their initial voyage was probably another deterring factor. For the most part, however, these were men with strong backs and big hearts. They were not quitters. Whatever life threw at them, they accepted because they truly believed that if they worked hard they could forge a future for themselves and their families. Slowly they adjusted to the climate. They fought for better working conditions and their relentless work ethic and determination eventually won the respect of all Canadians.

Today those Italian immigrants are fully integrated, prosperous and, especially, proud to be Canadians. Some who arrived as almost illiterate, unskilled laborers within a few years became masters of trades. Their productivity and skills were appreciated and valued. Many became contractors. Others built houses and, later, high-rises, and some became big land developers and are among the wealthiest people in Canada.

Similarly, those who went to work in factories often started their own manufacturing enterprises, creating jobs for thousands of Canadians. Still others opened commercial businesses such as fashion boutiques, beauty salons, and restaurants. Italian customs and tastes for wine, pizza, and espresso coffee became part of Toronto's culture and helped to change the city from a sleepy Victorian town to a truly cosmopolitan city.

All these people were true nation builders and their contribution to the Canadian economy and culture is beyond question today. Ironically, under current rules, most, if not all, of these men and women would not be allowed to immigrate to Canada today. The law now requires knowledge of an official language and a higher education.

Let me emphasize here that I am describing the experience of Italians from about the end of the Second World War to the late 1960s. I am not directly familiar with the experience of people from other parts of Europe who also came to Canada but it is fair to assume they encountered similar situations. Thanks to all their hard work, sacrifices, abilities, and knowledge, Canada today enjoys a strong economy. Those millions of poorly educated, non-English-speaking immigrants laid a solid economic foundation for Canada, which in turn funded all the benefits we enjoy today through our social welfare and health care systems.

Those early immigrants came to Canada asking nothing of the government. They paid for their own health care and their own homes. Public housing was unknown at the time. Yet they were grateful to Canada for the opportunity they were granted to make a new and better life here, and they remain so today.

Many of the older immigrants may resent more recent waves of immigrants when they complain they have it tough. Newcomers to Canada these days can often find public housing and they have access to one of the best socialized medical systems in the world. The only complaint from some is that they have to be three months in the country before they qualify. They are also protected from open discrimination by new human rights legislation that is strictly enforced, and they are shielded from abuse in the workplace by labour laws backed by stiff fines for violations. Each wave of immigrants should thank those who came before them for blazing the trail. None of the improvements they enjoy happened by accident.

I point this out simply to illustrate how far Canada and Ontario have progressed in what really has been a short period of time. It took only a generation or two to secure social justice and benefits for all. It reinforces for me the belief that this great country is one of the best, if not the best in the world.

CHAPTER 2

THE SAND HOG TRAGEDY

Shortly after I arrived, my sister and I moved to a flat on the third floor of a house on Clarence Avenue, just north of College Street in Toronto's west end. My sister was working at the bank and I had worked at various menial jobs for a few months. By Christmastime, I realized that without proper knowledge of the English language, my opportunities were going to remain limited. So in January 1960, my brother, who had moved to North Bay as a house builder, came back for a few days and drove me to Humberside Collegiate in Toronto, where my cousin Adriana was attending grade eleven. I was nineteen and so of high school age. The principal was sympathetic to me and assigned me classes: geography, history, and grade-thirteen English composition and literature. These were his choices. We studied *Hamlet*, and my head was spinning by the end of the class. It was all Greek to me. Slowly, however, the language became clearer and my English improved.

After classes I would go to my uncle Angelo Burigana's house on Perth Avenue where I started my education on a whole different front: union politics. Little did I know at the time that I would be learning a business from masters and that it would set the stage for my career. Uncle Angelo was a business agent for the Operative Plasterers and Cement Mason International Union, Local 117.

In North America, unions are usually structured as national or international bodies, based in either Canada or the United States. The national or international entity would then charter local unions, assigning them a number, a geographical area, and jurisdiction over specific trades. For example, the Hod Carriers and Common Laborers International Union of North America, later known simply as Laborers International Union of North America (LIUNA), chartered the LIUNA Local 183 in 1952, assigning its jurisdiction as all of Ontario and those labourers employed by Ontario Hydro. Uncle Angelo's Operative Plasterers and Cement Mason International Union, Local 117, represented plasterers and was the only trade in the residential housing sector to be unionized. Uncle Angelo was also an opera singer but in Canada he had had to learn the plastering trade. He was a good friend of Bruno Zanini, a bricklayer and another opera lover and singer who had made friends and enemies while organizing residential bricklayers into a short-lived union in the mid-1950s.

At the head of my uncle's Operative Plasterers and Cement Mason International Union in Canada was a Scottish immigrant, Charlie Irvine. He was a patriarch, tall, bony, with white hair and a personality that demanded respect. He was also the Canadian vice-president of his international union. At that time, he controlled four locals in Toronto, two for the plasterers (commercial and residential) and two for the cement masons, one still in existence today.

Irvine was a secretive person. He did not like offices and he often checked into hotel rooms under assumed names. He also carried on some business from my uncle Angelo's living room. His dream was to organize all "mud" trades (labourers, carpenters, bricklayers, cement masons, plasters) in the residential sector in Toronto, where the immigrants, mostly Italians, were working. He had strong connections with the international unions based in Washington, DC, and was able to persuade the Carpenters International, the Labourers International, and the Painters International to be part of a group of union locals under his guidance intent on organizing the residential construction industry.

Being in my uncle's house I was able to hear their conversations not so much by design as by proximity. I remember a heated discussion between Irvine and Windsor-based Sam Sasso, the Canadian vice-president for the Bricklayers International Union. Sasso strongly objected to Zanini being part of the group. Zanini, again, made a lot of enemies. Irvine made it clear that he would do without the Bricklayers Union but not without Zanini. In the end, however, Irvine conceded, and assigned Zanini to take charge of the Labourers Local.

Irvine started to call mass meetings in the evenings and weekends by distributing pamphlets on the job. These meetings were held at the Italo Canadian Recreation Club on Brandon Avenue and because of that the unions and locals that resulted became known as the Brandon Hall Group. I attended many of these gatherings with my uncle. They were crowded with Italian immigrants tired of being exploited, tired of working in despicable conditions. To call the meetings to order Irvine used his legendary "shillelagh": an Irish walking stick, also known as a fighting stick since it is robust and has a big knobby handle which is useful as a cudgel and effective in settling disputes. Irvine's speeches were not the firebrand type but they were well received when he spoke about working conditions and the necessity of the union. Zanini translated Irvine's speeches into Italian. His Italian was not very correct but it was what the people wanted to hear. He was a born performer.

It was not long after I arrived and the Brandon Hall Group started gaining traction that an unspeakable tragedy occurred. It would change everything.

On March 17, 1960, a crew of six Italians, nicknamed "sand hogs" because they tunnelled through the sand which lies under most of Toronto, were working at a Hogg's Hollow water-main tunnel in the Yonge Street and York Mills area. The conditions were cramped and dangerous. They had no helmets or flashlights. Because they were working under the Don River, there was danger of flooding. The ground was soft and silt-like so there was always an air compressor running to maintain a positive pressure in the six-foot-deep tunnel and to push any rising water back down. The downside was that all that air created an oxygen-rich environment and when a cutting torch ignited the rubber insulation on an electrical cable a fire spread quickly and with ferocious intensity. Soon the tunnel filled with toxic smoke. Five of the six sand hogs perished: Pasquale Allegrezza, Giovanni Battista Carriglio, Giovanni Fusillo and brothers Alessandro and Guido Mantella.

Some fifty years later, Vince Versace of the *Daily Commercial News*, a construction industry newspaper, described the chain of events in a story published on March 16, 2010:

> *Deadly fumes filled the tunnel, trapping five of six men working there. When emergency personnel turned off an air compressor to stop feeding the flames, silt and water filled the tunnel, sealing the fate of the five men inside.*
>
> *Jack Harrop Construction was originally responsible for the project but it [had experienced] "financial difficulties," city officials said at the time, and a trust company had taken over the job.*
>
> *There were six men in the tunnel when a cutting torch ignited the rubberized electrical cable it was attached to. Once the fire started, it roared off in the oxygen-rich environment, further fuelled by oil residue courtesy of the poorly serviced air compressor, an inquest would reveal.*
>
> *Deadly fumes filled the cavern. One worker managed to escape, but the other five could not see their way to safety. In order to avoid noxious fumes, they ran from the lone exit, blocked by fire, and*

headed towards the opposite end of the tunnel which ended at a concrete bulkhead 300 feet away. Before making that fateful walk towards the bulkhead one man had almost made it out, foreman Charles Valentini told a Toronto Daily Star reporter at the scene.

"I held one of their hands. I had to let go because of the heat. It was hell."

Investigators found that no fire extinguishers, resuscitator masks, or flashlights were in the tunnel, nor [was] any telephone system set up. When emergency personnel turned off the air compressor, in order to stop feeding the flames oxygen, they sealed the fate of the five men underground. With no pressure, water and silt started to seep in, filling the tunnel and piling up near the bulkhead, where the workers would later be found. An inquest would reveal some of the workers had water and silt in their lungs, pointing to an excruciating drowning death.

Buchinski, 26 at the time, was one of four men who volunteered for a rescue effort.

He had once worked with "some of the boys" who were trapped. The confined conditions in the tunnel meant rescuers had to squirm their way through heavy amounts of silt and water.

"We went in just over 100 feet. It was dark and there was a lot of water. We found one body lying over top of the pipe," recalls Buchinski sombrely. "We went by him for another 20 feet and then found all the silt piled high, maybe a foot from the ceiling of the tunnel."

Buchinski remembers to this day the chaos and pain that awaited them above ground once they emerged with the one deceased worker they found.

"It was a hard thing to do, there were hundreds of people there with so much family of those guys," he says. "When I came up, I did not want to be the one to say it was hopeless. We said things like 'We don't know', 'We did not go to the end,' and 'They could be on the other side of the silt.'"

Buchinski was plagued with nightmares for years after the incident. The helplessness he felt that night is still very real today.

"I didn't know what I was getting into," says Buchinski during an interview at his west Toronto home. "It was at night and I didn't even know it was under the river. We were stupid to go into a place like that in those conditions."

The Italian community reacted at first with sorrow but their sorrow quickly gave way to other emotions. Anger at the injustice and poor treatment of workers had been growing for some time. Every day many immigrant workers risked their lives in horrendous conditions and sometimes all they had to show for it after a month's work was a worthless piece of paper because some contractor's cheque had bounced. The terrible tragedy was a call for action and more voices started to shout out. The anger boiled over into rage.

"This disaster is one more illustration of the high cost a great city pays for its growth and the role the Italian-born builder has played on the development of Toronto," thundered a *Toronto Daily Star* editorial.

Over at the *Toronto Telegram*, labour reporter Frank Drea, who would go on to be a Member of Provincial Parliament and cabinet minister under Conservative Premier Bill Davis, wrote a series of stories highlighting the deplorable treatment of immigrant construction workers and detailing the growth of union activism in the Italian construction community.

These stories pulled no punches. "Hell Hole" blared the *Toronto Telegram* in massive front-page type, on March 18, 1960. "Slave Immigrants" it raged a week later, reflecting that the furious reaction of the public was not abating as the bodies were pulled to the surface. Drea's reporting noted immigrant workers were "treated like animals."

With publisher John Bassett's backing—he, too, was shocked at the working conditions—and despite pressure from rich land developers, the *Telegram* crusaded on these themes for two weeks until Premier Leslie Frost started to take notice of the shift in public sentiment. When the coroner's report came out, noting how safety rules had been brushed aside and how management had ignored the risks to the lives of workers, the clamour for change rose still higher. It had come to light that the Hogg's Hollow tunnel was a disaster in the making. A foreman who had voiced safety concerns had been fired. Another had quit, fearing a collapse because the tunnel was improperly built and there were no fire extinguishers.

The Ontario government was forced to act. Frost launched the Royal Commission on Industrial Safety, chaired by P. J. McAndrew, which found that despite the existence of safety legislation, "accident prevention associations are not functioning . . . as contemplated by the Act and . . . are isolated islands of autonomy having no responsibility to report to or even advise the Workmen's Compensation Board [now known as the Workplace Safety and Insurance Board]." Immediately things changed. Charlie Irvine's meetings started to fill with more and more workers who were sick and tired of their working conditions and ready to fight for their rights. And what a fight it would be.

CHAPTER 3

THE STRIKE OF 1960

I finished school in the spring of 1960 just after the Hogg's Hollow disaster. My uncle Angelo found me a job as a labourer for a plastering company owned by another Italian. The plan was for it to be a temporary placement until I found a better job.

So each day I showed up 6:00 a.m. at St. Clair Avenue West at Landsdowne Avenue, one of the major gathering points of the city where workers would wait for the arrival of the company pickup trucks. I traveled in the pickup truck's cabin for the first two days, next to the driver, but later on I was assigned to the back of the vehicle with the rest of the workers.

It was not comfortable. We sat on wooden benches under one of those dangerous plywood canopies with job tools like wheelbarrows and shovels loaded on the other half. These days, transportation of tools and passengers in unsegregated compartments is not allowed but back then it was the rule. On the first day I was assigned to the hod: a V-shaped mortar carrier with a long handle. The V-shaped load was held on the shoulder, with the handle in your hands in front of your body. It was some of the heaviest and most tiring work you could do but it was a commonplace job on a site, which is why the Labourers Union was initially called the Hod Carriers Union. By the middle of the 1960s, hod transportation made way for mechanized means and today the term "hod" is unknown to most people.

The plasterers came mainly from the Friuli–Venezia Giulia region of Italy, which is where I was born. Despite our common roots, they were merciless on the job, furiously yelling "mortar, mortar" when supplies ran low, and throwing in sonorous swear words in the Friulian dialect. The pace they set was backbreaking. It was as if they were machines. I doubt you could find men with that kind of stamina today. After two hours humping that hod the foreman had pity on me. I was a skinny boy, weighing just 145 pounds on a beanpole frame, standing about six feet tall. They assigned me to clean up debris.

Over my first two weeks on the job I continued to participate in Irvine's union meetings, which were open to all construction workers. One Sunday, Irvine thundered from the stage: "Tomorrow we go on strike, boys!"

Both Irvine and the Italian workers, who were not aware of Canadian regulations, could not have cared less whether the strike was legal or not. In Ontario, a strike can be declared only when a collective agreement has expired or a certification is granted by the Ontario Labour Relations Board. In both cases, a government conciliation procedure, which can last many months, must take place before authorization for the strike is received from the Ministry of Labour. Still, this was no time for rules. Italian workers would descend into the streets because they were tired of being exploited, working in precarious conditions with serious safety problems and meagre salaries. This action had been brewing for months and the deaths of the Hogg's Hollow workers merely accelerated things.

Thousands backed the strike declared by Irvine, despite their need to pay their mortgages, feed their families, and meet other financial burdens. It was a huge risk. The workers were new to Canada, and they were just coming off winter unemployment when the strike began. It would require enormous personal sacrifices to see it through.

In his book, *The Italians Who Built Toronto: Italian Workers and Contractors in the City's Housebuilding Industry, 1950–1980*, Stefano Agnoletto, a Milanese professor who studied at the University of Toronto, noted that in the 1950s and '60s between 50 and 60 per cent of the construction workers in Toronto had Italian roots. Italians were the lowest-paid ethnic group in Toronto, with the men making an average wage of about $4,520 a year while Italian women earned only half of that.

Every morning during the dispute, Brandon Hall's flying squads of one or two hundred strikers would go to various rendez-vous points to convince other workers to abstain from working. Later in the day, these same teams would go from job site to job site, trying to convince those who were working to join the strike. Some, mainly non-Italians, opposed the action and on more than one occasion bricks and two-by-fours were used against the flying squads. Police were often called to restore order and sometimes to make arrests.

The strike was front-page news for weeks. The *Telegram's* Frank Drea, who had whipped up passions with his crusade fol-lowing the Hogg's Hollow disaster, was again out front on this story, helping to rally public opinion to our cause. I was nineteen years old and leading one of the flying squads. I had also signed up more than 2,000 labourers for the new Local Union 811 of the Hod Carriers and Common Labourers International Union during the meetings at Brandon Hall. I was one of the ten found-ing members of that local, the eighth signature. The head was my uncle Angelo's old friend Bruno Zanini. All that was required to join was a dollar and a signature. During that period, other trade unionists were also making headway. Nick Gileno of the labourers, Frank Colantonio of the carpenters, Marino Toppan and Mike Hammer of the bricklayers, Tony Mariano of the cement finishers, and many others belonging to various trades were all signing up new members from a workforce sick of being exploited.

The strike required our full commitment for seven weeks, day and night. Irvine paid each one of us $80 out of his own pocket but for only a week. After seven weeks of hard struggle and continuous confrontation on the job sites and in the face of the great solidarity of the strikers, the employers gave in. By that time, residential construction had practically come to a standstill. The majority of the contractors in each trade (bricklayers, carpenters, cement finishers, painters) signed a collective agreement with the locals representing their trades. The new hourly rate and working conditions were close to those in the commercial sector. It was a great conquest, although, as we will see later on, it lasted like the snow in an April sun. Within a few years, everything fell apart.

There were, however, palpable benefits which laid the groundwork for future unionization and contracts. Many of these immigrant workers were for the first time represented by a union, their hourly rate greatly improved, and reasonable working hours finally established in a collective agreement. There was also a grievance process to remedy employers' violations and to protect employers from employees who broke the terms of the collective agreement. The strike of 1960 was not a strike as we know it. The Italian immigrants did not fight just for money or better working conditions. They fought primarily for their dignity. They wanted respect. They were tired of being pushed around by almost everybody, including the police, who treated us like animals. They wanted to be treated as Canadian citizens. Irvine decided he wanted the new union members to march in the Labour Day Parade at the Canadian National Exhibition grounds in 1960. I have to give him credit for the idea, because I acted as a marshal for the event and I still remember the pride in the workers' faces as they marched for the first time as equals.

Shortly after the Labour Day weekend, Zanini told me he no longer needed me. The strike was over and he gave my job as secretary of Local 811 to a relative, even though this man had never worked in the industry: he had been a window cleaner and continued to work as one during the strike. I was upset and I went to Irvine asking for his intervention. Irvine spoke to Zanini, asking him to explain his decision and reconsider. We were in the small library of Brandon Hall and Irvine and Zanini were standing in a corner of the room. I was at the other end. After a long conversation, Irvine said in a loud voice: "Okay, Bruno, do whatever you want, but one day you will regret it," a prophecy that would come true.

Nevertheless, I was now out of a job. I got by when Charles Caccia, who went on to be elected to Parliament, lent me $25 to carry me over. The months of October and November were very hard. I had no work, no money, and I was alone since my sister had married and moved to North Bay. I was too proud to ask my brother or sister for money and so at the end of November I went to the Labourers headquarters, Local 183, run by Gerry Gallagher. I had never met Gallagher before. He was an Irish immigrant and a militant from the ranks of the Labour Party in England, and a great speaker.

In Toronto, there were two other Labourers locals besides Gallagher's Local 183, which had about 1,000 members. The new Local 811, with Zanini at its head, had about 2,000 members, and Local 506, which represented the labourers of the commercial and residential sectors, had almost 5,000 members. The three locals were branches of the Labourers International Union of North America.

Local 183 had been founded in 1952, during the Cold War, when the threat of nuclear attack by Communist Russia was alive in everyone's minds. Left-leaning unions were viewed unfavourably by governments because they seemed to be linked to the ideas of the Communist Party and were thus taken as a threat to national security. It was in this context that the Seafarers' International Union had conspired with the federal government in

1949 to purge the ranks of the Communist-dominated Canadian Seamen's Union. The man they tasked with the job was an American, Hal C. Banks. Using muscle, intimidation, beatings, and murder, Banks and his goons eliminated the CSU and brought in the SIU. The Canadian labour movement was shocked and out-raged. The SIU was expelled from the Canadian Labour Congress and condemned by a Royal Commission. (Banks was eventually indicted for assaulting a rival leader and forced to flee Canada for the United States where he was sheltered by Washington. President Lyndon B. Johnson refused to honour an extradition request from the Lester B. Pearson government.) According to Gerry Gallagher, Ontario Hydro officials went to Washington in the early 1950s to meet with the Building Trades Department of the American Federation of Labor and Congress of Industrial Organizations (AFL-CIO). Hydro wanted help setting up a construction union that would have no communists in its ranks. As a result, the Laborers International Union, a member of the AFL-CIO, was invited to represent construction workers in Ontario under LIUNA charter Local 183.

Gallagher, a labourer working for Ontario Hydro in the Burlington area, was hired as a full-time union representative for Local 183. He traveled to all projects of Ontario Hydro in the province, regardless of how remote, and signed up close to 2,000 laborers employed by the utility. He appointed union stewards at every "line and station" to better service the members. Before long he was elected as secretary treasurer of the local, which at that time was the top position. Gallagher was no patsy. When Ontario Hydro started to sublet work to cable-laying contractors, taking away work from union members, Gallagher successfully organized a number of cable-laying firms as "utilities contrac-tors." This also covered contractors primarily laying cable for Bell Telephone.

The advent of Local 183 caused problems with other labourer locals in Ontario, all of which were protective of their jurisdiction.

After a long period of infighting and complaints to their international parent, Local 183 traded its provincial mandate for a reduced Toronto mandate, but in return it was granted jurisdiction over all subway and road sewer and water-main construction. Gallagher knew from his experience in London, England, that subway construction was not a one-time project but a perennial job creator. Toronto's University line subway construction started shortly afterwards as a union project. Local 183 represented both the labourers in the so-called open-cut subway construction and the muckers and miners in the tunnel sections. All the other trades were represented by other construction unions.

The problem with Gallagher's deal was that roads, and sewer and water-main construction companies were mainly non-union. Most labourers were Italian immigrants and Gallagher needed to organize them. Serendipitously, this was right about the time I showed up. After my bitter experience with Bruno Zanini, I was flat broke and unable to pay rent. Somebody told me about Local 183 so I went to the local office on Bond Street, just north of Queen Street in Toronto. It was a three-room office, one room for Gerry Gallagher, another for the two secretaries and record keeping, and a third that served as a small reception area for members.

Gallagher welcomed me and asked me all sorts of questions, in particular about my experience with the Brandon Hall Group and Zanini. I was open and frank with Gallagher. At the end he said that he would recommend hiring me as a union organizer to the local executive board, which had the hiring authority, at a meeting the following week. At the time the board was composed of mostly Irish miners working in subway construction.

A week after my conversation with Gallagher, I read my horoscope in the *Toronto Daily Star*; it told me: "Tomorrow you will begin work for a social organization." The phone rang half an hour later. It was Gallagher: "You can start tomorrow." I still remember that "tomorrow" was December 6, 1960. Years later, Gallagher told me he had received a number of phone calls from the Brandon Hall representatives asking him not to hire me because I was a troublemaker and a communist. I had no idea where they got that from. Luckily, Gallagher did not trust them and, in particular, he did not like Zanini.

CHAPTER 4

MY START WITH LOCAL 183

was hired as a union organizer, to sign up and unionize labourers working for non-union road, and sewer and water-main contractors. My first day on the job, Gallagher outlined my weekly pay and benefits. My salary was $90 a week plus car expenses. I must have put on a funny face because Gerry apologized and said that the local could not pay more. Inside, however, I was dancing with joy. It was like winning the lottery.

The membership in the local at that time was around 1,000, a much reduced number due mostly to its jurisdiction having been cut from province-wide to Toronto. I made myself familiar with the sewer and water-main industry—the road-building industry was shut down for the season—and got to work. I soon learned that workers for non-union contractors were afraid to join the union on the job site. They were even afraid to talk to me in the presence of their foreman, so I adopted a new strategy. Early in the morning I went to various assembly points through the city where the labourers were picked up by their bosses. Quickly, I wrote down their names and telephone numbers. In the evening

I would call them, get their addresses, and pay them visits. Most of them welcomed me into their homes, unafraid since they were not being seen or heard by their bosses.

It was hard work. Everyone insisted I try some homemade wine. They were so proud of their vino! Over drinks, I would explain to them the labour laws of the country and underline the secrecy of the process. To organize a company, the law required us to sign up at least 45 per cent of the employees in its bargaining unit, and to collect at least one dollar as a membership fee from each person who signed up, to force a vote. If, however, we signed up 65 per cent of the bargaining unit, certification was automatic. The payment of one dollar was crucial. If it was proven that just one worker had not paid the dollar, all applications for certification would be jeopardized at the Ontario Labour Relations Board (OLRB).

The first company I organized was Aprile Contracting. At the OLRB hearing, which at that time was compulsory, I was accompanied by Syd L. Robins, a well-respected lawyer with a soft side for the labour cause. He later became an Ontario Supreme Court Justice. I watched carefully, impressed by the legal ritual and the duel between the company lawyer and Robins. My second application was Marino Construction. This time, however, I found myself alone at the OLRB. Either our office or Robins' office had got the dates wrong. Regardless, I had to press on. The company lawyer tried to oppose the certification and I did my best to put forward our position remembering the legal niceties I had heard from Robins at the previous hearing. I must have done a good job because we won the case. Here I was, just twenty years old, only eighteen months in the country, and I was winning cases at a tribunal. A few years later, at a Christmas reception by the Teamsters Union at the Westbury Hotel, the chairman of the OLRB, Bill Reid, congratulated me on that presentation.

Slowly, the number of unionized companies increased. During the early spring of 1961, I concentrated on non-union road-building companies and servicing our members who worked for paving companies. I liked to do this over lunch. I would drop by union road-building sites, sit down with the union workers to hear their grievances, and then explain to them how the union structure in Canada was different from in Italy. The workers were kind to me and each time they went out of their way to offer me part of their lunch, which, out of respect, I ate. My organizing method was slow and the opposite of the Irvine-Zanini method, but mine was the legal way, like building on rock, not on sand, and over time I was proven right.

By winter of that year, Gallagher had hired another representative, Mike Reilly, who was a lead miner and president of the local. (The position of president under the local union constitution is an honorary one. He has the authority to chair meetings and co-sign cheques but the real authority rests with the business manager.) Mike was a good family man and he did not drink, an oddity for the Irishmen I knew at the time. We formed a strong team and became friends and I was named the godfather of his first son, his sixth child after five daughters.

That same winter I met Ed Boyer, a labour member of the OLRB. Boyer was living in Kitchener and asked me if he could stay in my flat two nights per week and pay his fair share. It turned out to be a blessing. Boyer was a carpenter who had become the Ontario Secretary Treasurer of the Carpenters Union before his appointment to the OLRB. He was a strong socialist, with roots in the Cooperative Commonwealth Federation, a left-leaning political party which was formed in Regina in 1933 and which, in 1961, would become the New Democratic Party. He knew a lot about the Canadian labour movement and he was happy to share what he knew. He told me that during the "lean years," David Lewis, a famous labour lawyer who later became leader of the NDP, would stay at his house in Kitchener because the fledgling CCF had so little money. Lewis's conversations with Ed were part of Ed's education and he passed the lessons on to me.

During the long winter nights, Ed would talk about politics, the Canadian labour movement, and, most of all, the Ontario Labour Relations Act, how it came into being, the reasons why many of the articles had been instituted, and the interpretation of them by the Ontario Labour Relations Board. It was like planting seeds in my mind. It took a number of years but slowly, surely, I started to understand the process. In time, with this background, I was successful in amending and promoting a number of the labour laws that the labour movement and, in particular, the building trade unions enjoy today.

At the time, I was also attending the weekly meeting of the Toronto Construction Building Trades Council, every Thursday morning at 10 a.m. at the Labour Temple on Church Street. The council was then very powerful and it coordinated the activities of construction locals of various trades, primarily in the so-called Industrial Commercial Institutional (ICI) sector, since the others were mainly non-union. The manager was Albert Hall, a very imposing figure and a dedicated trade unionist. The meetings were attended by about fifty full-time business agents from various trades, all of them grey-haired and battle hardened. I remember them looking at me with sympathy and compassion, if not commiseration. I was but twenty and had just arrived from another country. Listening to them, I learned more about the trade. They were great Canadians, true pioneers, and dedicated to the movement with a passion we do not see today. They had all taken their lumps for the cause through many years of struggle. I had been through one major strike but I was about to earn my wings in a way I never saw coming.

CHAPTER 5

ARRESTED ON
THE JOB

The strike of 1960 was a major victory but it was just one battle in a still raging war. Irvine succeeded in getting the majority of contractors in each trade to sign a collective agreement but failed to get the house and apartment builders to do the same. The hourly rates and working conditions were improved, although perhaps too fast for comfort. The builders continued to sublet their work to cheaper bids, most of them submitted by non-union contractors. Many union contractors learned to simply change their names and become non-union shops, or they just ignored the collective agreement.

At the time, before Ontario labour legislation was amended, shutting down one company and emerging with a new company under a different name was an easy dodge to avoid a collective agreement. To start a new business in the residential construction industry required little capital. All you needed was an old pickup truck, a few wheelbarrows, some shovels and other tools. The upshot was that the progress made after a long and bitter strike was fading within a year. The fatal mistake Irvine and the

Brandon Hall Group made was a lack of flexibility and an inability to listen to the other side. The union contractors pleaded with them to reopen the collective agreements because they felt the newly established rates were too high and they could not compete against the non-union employers. They were asking for more flexibility but the answer was always no. Instead, in the spring of 1961, Irvine and Zanini called for weekly evening meetings to prepare the workers for another strike. Gallagher asked me to participate in these meetings, both to observe and to assist.

I invited Ed Boyer to come along with me to one of these assemblies and he was disappointed at what we saw and heard. One night after we got home he said, "They will end up going nowhere and they will have a sad end." I asked why and he said because they were acting outside the law. "The law is the law even if we don't like it and it is necessary to know how to use it to one's advantage," said Boyer.

At the end of May 1961, Irvine and Zanini called a second strike, hoping a new show of force would solve a situation that was degenerating rapidly. Gallagher asked me once again to give a hand but I was firmly against the Brandon Hall Group's program and I explained to him that I had no trust in the Irvine-Zanini method. I tried to make him understand that, all things considered, Local 183 had nothing to do with the dispute or with the group and we could stay out of it. Moreover, I had always acted according to the law and our employers lived up to our collective agreements. Contractors respected our collective agreements because they were realistic. We never tried to catch up to the higher rates of the ICI. We reflected the reality of our industry. Gallagher agreed but was adamant: "You're right. But we have to make the effort to help out the workers." Since the majority of those workers were Italian, I felt I had to accept that decision.

And so it began again. At 6 a.m., I would go to Brandon Hall and join the convoys going to various job sites to picket. At one point, Gallagher tasked Reilly and me to stop the subway construction, a job at the time being run by the Perini-Kiewit company which was doing the open cuts, with Robert McAlpine Ltd. doing the tunnelling.

Reilly went to the tunnel section and I went to the open cut. At 7 a.m., I walked from Union Station up University Avenue to Dundas Street, along the way asking our members to stop working in solidarity with the residential construction workers. Most of them were new to Canada and felt a stoppage was against their interest since the labour dispute had nothing to do with them. Still, out of loyalty to the local union, they obliged, laid down their tools, and walked off the job. The general superintendent of the subway project, Ettore Faccini, an older Italian immigrant with great skills, was well respected by the workers. He tried to intervene and stop the walkout. Many of them were his friends and *paesani*, or countrymen, but my plea prevailed. Gallagher's tactic generated big publicity in the news media because the subway construction was the most important project in Toronto.

On the morning of June 1, 1961, I was in a strikers' convoy, as usual, heading off to do what had become routine. Another member of Local 183, Angelo Scopelliti, who was working in the subway tunnel, joined me. I was driving my own car and there were two other strikers with us. We left from the Brandon Hall office at St. Clair and Lansdowne, heading east towards the various rendezvous points where the workers waited for the company vehicles to pick them up.

This strike was not like the one a year earlier. It had become nasty and there was violence on both sides. Sometimes the strikers would physically block workers from going to work, or working construction workers would throw bricks and two-by-fours at the strikers. As we drove along, I noticed a police cruiser coming up on us and I told Scopelliti that I was breaking away from the main group, going my own way. While the main group went east on St. Clair Avenue, I headed north on Dufferin Street where we came upon a small group on their way to work. We stopped. Without getting out of the car, I asked them why they had not joined the strike in progress. They said they were members of the Bricklayers Local 2, a group from the commercial construction sector which was not involved in the strike.

I asked for their union membership cards and they produced them and everything was good so we were saying "Ciao" when suddenly we were surrounded by three police cruisers. A police officer pulled me out of the car, illegally searched me, and made me open the trunk. Now, this kind of action by the police was and still is illegal but, of course, then and now, police simply deny that they do such things. They made me open up the trunk and they searched the vehicle as a big group of workers who were going to their factory jobs gathered around us, watching the scene. The sergeant gave me an order which I did not quite understand at first because of the general confusion around us and the fear that had overwhelmed me. I had never been confronted by the cops before and my English was not perfect. As I asked for clarifications about what I was supposed to do, the sergeant, a huge man, well built, grabbed me by the lapels and flung me into his cruiser and I found myself under arrest for obstructing the police.

I was taken to the police station and released on bail with the assistance of a union lawyer. The judge ordered me to keep away from the strike but there was no way I was going to follow orders, especially after that incident, and so I continued the struggle. It was only later when I went to court that I realized how serious my situation was.

The strike went on for six weeks and it was front-page news every day in the *Toronto Star,* the *Telegram,* and the *Globe and Mail.* Many of these stories talked about the strike's violence, which was not as serious as they described it. Mostly the incidents were confrontations of angry men. Some wanted to work and, like most of us, needed the money to support their families. On the other hand, the strikers were passionately striving to improve everyone's wages and working conditions and they were angry that those who continued to work would themselves benefit from the improvements eventually but were prolonging the strike. The home builders' groups, who were politically well connected at the federal, provincial, and municipal levels, called on the government to deport non-Canadian strikers involved in violent actions. These outrageous comments naturally made headlines. The situation was tense and there were still a minority of workers, non-Italians mostly, who did not adhere to the strike.

While the violence was generally overstated, there were several serious incidents. One morning, at around 11 a.m., I found myself at Brandon Hall when one of the strikers, Albino Petta, came in with his head gushing blood. A Polish bricklayer had cracked his head with a brick, he said, but he refused to go to the hospital or see a doctor because he was afraid of being deported. I told him not to worry and took him to a doctor immediately. At the end of the strike, I transferred Albino from the Local Union 811 to our Local Union 183 and I sent him to work on the construction of the subway where the work was safer and better paid. He remained there for many years. Albino was a good man from the Abruzzi region of Italy and, in gratitude, he asked me to be the godfather at the baptism of his first-born son.

Back to the summer of 1961. It was a rough six weeks. More than a hundred people were arrested over the duration and in just one day police arrested forty strikers. The day after that mass arrest I had to go to court for my hearing. Instead of having my case put over until the strike ended to let emotions subside, my lawyer made the mistake of pressing ahead. The police officer who testified against me in court shamelessly lied. The sergeant insisted he had heard me incite forty strikers to violence and said that on being told to disperse I yelled at the group to ignore him. My lawyer asked how forty people could have travelled in two cars. The sergeant could not answer. Nor could he remember if I was talking to them in English or Italian. Finally, he blurted out that I was speaking in Italian.

So, my lawyer asked the sergeant, do you speak Italian? No, he did not.

"Then how do you know what Stefanini said?" my lawyer demanded. Again, the policeman could not explain.

I clearly remember the judge nodding off even as my lawyer was summarizing my case in his final address. As soon as we wrapped up our defence, the judge perked up. He had clearly made up his mind: "The purpose of the jail term is to deter others. Six months of jail time."

I was stunned. Even the Crown Attorney came over and shook both my hand and his head: "I'm sorry, a two-weeks jail sentence would have been good enough for me."

The next thing I knew, I was off to jail where, on the second day, a federal immigration official came to see me and made no secret of why he was there. "We don't want people like you in this country," he snarled at me. "We will send you back to Italy." The next day, I was moved to the maximum security section where the most dangerous criminals were locked up because, with deportation hanging over me, I was now a flight risk.

Sadness assailed me in jail. I felt alone. On my second day, I was sitting on a bench along the corridor of the dormitory when I was approached by somebody saying something to me. In my state of mind, I did not even listen to what he was saying and I did not answer. This made him angrier and he loomed over me as if to attack me. Suddenly, a voice from the other end of the corridor thundered: "Dumb nigger, leave the kid alone!"

While this kind of language would probably trigger a race riot in a jail today, back then it was commonplace. Just as we were called wops and dagos, blacks were openly called niggers. It was not right but it was the way it was. The man stopped instantly and walked away without protest. I figured I should go and at least meet and thank my protector. He was a medium-built man, about forty years old and, as it turned out, Italian. He spoke to me cordially: "Don't worry, kid, nobody will touch you as long as you are here."

I thanked him, adding that I did not know his name. "But I know you," he replied, and he showed me the newspaper from a couple of days before where on the front page was my photograph and a big headline: "Strike-Union Leader Jailed Six Months." He had just received the newspaper. To get a newspaper in jail, detainees had to order it a few days in advance and their name would be written at the top of the paper. And that is how I figured out my protector's name was John Papalia, also known as Johnny Pops. I still have that newspaper today. Now, this was a big deal both inside and outside the joint. Johnny Pops was a Hamilton-based organized-crime boss. The man was connected, and the kind of guy you respected and did not mess with. I had never heard of him and I never met him again because in a few days I was granted bail, pending my appeal.

While I was in jail there had been a mass rally of 16,000 construction workers from all sectors at the Canadian National Exhibition grounds. It was organized by the Toronto Building and Construction Trades Council and the Brandon Hall Group as a show of strength to get the government's attention and urge its intervention. Gallagher took advantage of the rally and spoke of my case with words to this effect: "It's a shame that this poor Italian boy, who is just twenty years old, has been sentenced to six months in jail just for having defended his people."

Gallagher's oration inflamed the crowd and when he finished everyone stood up and applauded for a long time, screaming for my release. With me having become a popular cause, the union hired Arthur Maloney, considered to be one of the best defence lawyers money could buy, to defend me. He had defended members of the notorious Boyd Gang. He went on to be both a Member of Parliament and an Ontario Member of Provincial Parliament and he was the first Ontario Ombudsman, from 1975 to 1979.

Maloney's first move was to get me released on bail. Two Canadian trade unionists whom I did not know and who were extraneous to the dispute—Scotty Lines, the president of the Labourers Local 506, and Stan Newmarch, the business manager of the Plumbers Local 46 in Toronto—mortgaged their houses in order to post my bail. The Crown demanded property as an assurance since a cash bail would just have been a deposit with the rest owed. Given that I faced deportation, they wanted to make sure I did not take off—although how could I? Canada was now my home. Later, when I found out what the two men had done for me, I was very grateful and I continue to be grateful to this day to these two outstanding trade unionists.

Eventually I learned why I had been jailed. It turned out that Irvine and Zanini had met with Premier Leslie Frost. They had reached a general agreement: in exchange for an end to the strike, the government would set up a Royal Commission to identify the problems faced by construction workers in the residential sector and to propose new legislation. Despite this agreement being in place, Irvine and Zanini went from the premier's office to a members' meeting at the Lansdowne Theatre and urged the strikers to intensify their actions. The retribution was swift. The following day, forty strikers were arrested, and the day after that was my court appearance. I was in the wrong place at the wrong time when a strong message was about to be delivered.

While the union supported me, the harshness of my sentence was a cold shower for the strikers. They feared that if they continued to picket, they, too, would be arrested. They were scared to go on. As a result, the strike dissolved and within two years the Brandon Hall Group no longer existed. The Bricklayers Local Union 40 detached itself. Administrative control of the Labourers Local 811 was taken over by the International Union due to irregularities around the use of funds and after a few more years it disappeared. The residential Carpenters Local Union of the Brandon Hall Group lost a lot of members and was transferred to the Carpenters Union Toronto office. The painters left the Brandon Hall Group and later, led by Armando Colafranceschi, slowly recovered and flourished again after a few years.

An unrelated but similarly devastating development for the Brandon Hall Group was that Irvine's plasterers were annihilated by the introduction of drywall into construction technology. In those days, walls were framed with wooden two-by-four studs. Then a system of thin wood strips or metal mesh was tacked to the studs. With that in place, up to three coats of plaster would be put on, like icing a cake. It was labour intensive but it allowed for more creative décor, such as round shapes or arches. It was also slightly better for soundproofing. Drywall, made of gypsum sandwiched between sheets of paper, had been introduced in the 1960s and it was faster, smoother, and more efficient to work with. It took over the business, meaning the old lathe and plaster guys either adapted to the new materials or they did not find much work. Seeing the threat to his plasterers, Irvine fought tooth and nail against drywall. He soon found, though, that you cannot stop progress and that one man's misfortune is another's gain. Seeing the future, a small trade union headed by a young Italian named Agostino (Gus) Simone jumped on the drywallers' trade and organized it. Simone was another good man from the Abruzzi region of Italy. He had originally represented the lathers. Drywall, however, was going to be big and he knew it.

The Government of Ontario kept its commitment and appointed the Royal Commission on Labour-Management Relations in the Construction Industry under H. Carl Goldenberg. He was assisted by a University of Toronto professor, John Crispo, who to my great surprise, on an autumn evening in 1961, invited me to his house on Avenue Road, north of Eglinton Avenue West, to chat informally. We talked extensively about problems in the residential construction industry and I immediately felt at ease. He asked me a lot of questions and I did my best to make him understand the conditions that workers toiled under. I had just turned twenty-one and I did not know the Canadian legislative system well enough to suggest how to modify the law. Still, bit by bit, I was learning and when I managed to master it, I would be in a position to propose a number of laws and to change others to the benefit of the workers' cause.

In 1962, the Goldenberg Commission presented its report. It had heard extensive evidence on how owners used shell companies to circumvent the Labour Relations Act. As I noted earlier, they would just change the name of the front company, leave the same people running things, and void the collective agreement. The workers were left with no union and no protection. Goldenberg got right to the point: "It is clear that the situation as described, and which I find to be a correct statement of the facts, is not conducive to peaceful industrial relations." He made a specific recommendation to amend the Ontario Labour Relations Act: "Consideration should be given to measures for the protection of acquired bargaining rights in situations arising from certain types of business practices which may affect such rights, for example, where a contractor, engaged on a number of projects in each of which he has a different partner, is in a position to shift employees from a project with respect to which certification has been granted to another."

This was finally done but it took nine more years. In 1971, the Ontario Labour Relations Act was changed through the Davis Amendments. Ultimately, however, nothing really changed for the workingman.

CHAPTER 6

AN ALTAR BOY
IN PRISON

From July 1961 to February 1962 I continued to organize non-union workers until at 5 a.m. on February 13 my room-mate, Ed Boyer, woke me up and joked: "Time to go to jail!" My lawyer was going to argue my appeal in court and the process required that I surrender myself into custody before court opened. The arguments seemed to go on forever as I waited in the cells. Then, about 5 p.m., a guard came down and told me I would now go to prison for three months instead of six. I was shocked and bewildered. Although three was better than six, I had expected more clemency from the court since things had settled down. We were not able to present any new evidence or arguments because in an appeal we could only argue the defence we had already made and show that the original trial judge had made an error. My original case had been poorly prepared and that hurt me. My friend Mike Reilly from Local 183 sat in the courtroom during the appeal and said one of the three judges on the panel seemed determined to send a message. "This case reminds me of what happened in Argentina recently [when a brawl broke out during a soccer game]," the judge said. "These people have to learn that we have laws here that have to be respected."

It was a sad day for me. I wanted to cry but my pride held me back. I noticed, however, that not too far from me another prisoner *was* crying. He was about thirty-five years old and, as I discovered, Italian. He, too, had been picked up in a mass arrest during the strike of 1961. By coincidence, his hearing was on the same day as my appeal. He had been given a month in jail and was crying because he was worried about his family. They would have no money coming in. He poured out his emotions: "Who is going to feed my family?"

It was a tough moment for both of us. Coincidentally, twenty years later I hired the man's son, John Colacci, as a trade union representative. John had graduated from Ryerson and worked in construction. I also promoted him as the director of the Local 183 Training Centre which I established years later. Though his hiring was a complete coincidence, I would never forget the tears of a father who was worried about his family. We all struggled to provide for our families. Being denied work, losing money due to a work-related injury, or being sent to jail for trying to stand up for your rights: these are injustices to all workers.

A few days after the hearing, I was moved from the Don Jail in Toronto to the Ontario Reformatory in Guelph. This was where young men with no previous criminal records and sentenced to less than two years of jail time were sent for rehabilitation. Those given more than six months were segregated in individual cells and subjected to aptitude tests before they were assigned to a skills-training program. The administration thought I had been given a nine-month sentence instead of three on appeal. I can only assume that they added three months to the original six instead of deducting. Before they figured out their mistake, I was examined by a psychologist who congratulated me for my intelligence quotient which he found to be above average. Once it was clear that I was only there for three months, I was moved to a dormitory where I learned the ropes.

I had been issued a new uniform of denim pants and jacket. Another detainee wanted to me to trade it to him for cigarettes and chocolate. I declined. He turned nasty and said, "I'll beat you up and take it off of you." I made the mistake of telling him that I would report him the guards. Being a northern Italian, it was what we did. Our culture reported any wrongdoing to the police. But I had no idea what I had triggered. Telling a guard was the worst thing that could be done in prison. Worse, I was vulnerable and exposed as I had been assigned to the kitchen because the threat of deportation was still hanging over me and the guards wanted to keep an eye on me. Unfortunately, the kitchen was also where the nastiest juvenile detainees were assigned. It was large with a three-storey ceiling. An observation tower rose from the centre with a guard perched inside to keep an eye on us. At one point, I noticed the detainees in the kitchen had formed a kind of human circle. Slowly, they were huddling around me. Some of them had knives, which were easy to come by in the kitchen. They had organized themselves so that the guard observing from above would not notice anything strange. When I realized what was going on I quickly jumped over to the observation tower's staircase and climbed up. The guard ordered me to go down but I refused, saying that I needed to be put into protective custody. He asked my name and called his bosses. After a while, two other guards arrived and transferred me to the infirmary where I felt safe.

My new job at the infirmary was nice. It was clean and calm and required little work. I learned to play chess and read a lot of books, including *The Conquest of Happiness* by the philosopher Bertrand Russell. I also won my first chess game, provoking anger in the man who taught me how to play. The majority of the guards had served in the British Army and leaned left, towards the Labour Party, so they were good to me. They knew why I was jailed and would secretly slip me new razor blades and other basic essential items. The prison chaplain even asked me to assist him as an altar boy during the Mass and it reminded me of my time as a young boy in Italy. At one point, I remembered all the excuses that I had made up for my parish priest who wanted me to be an altar boy. I almost burst out laughing at the thought of it. I had come all the way to a Canadian jail to be an altar boy.

During my sentence, an official from the Department of Immigration came to see me. He was much more cordial than the first man I had encountered. Still, he made me understand that I was at risk of being deported. That same week, Reilly also came to visit and I told him about the deportation threat. He told Gallagher. By coincidence, the Canadian Labour Congress convention, which occurred every two years, was to be held in Vancouver a week or so after my Immigration encounter. Gallagher went to the convention and spoke with the president of the CLC, Claude Jodoin, about my situation. Jodoin set up a meeting with Michael Starr, who was then the federal Labour minister, and who was at the convention representing his government. Starr promised Gallagher that he would look into my case but asked that the matter remain confidential.

The next day, just before Starr's speech to the convention, Jodoin asked Gallagher to bring up my case on the floor of the assembly in front of more than 2,000 delegates. Gallagher was reluctant because he had promised to keep the matter private. But Jodoin insisted and Gallagher relented. He was a great speaker. He used simple but human terms to portray my plight: "This poor Italian boy who looks like a student is in jail only for having defended the rights of Italian immigrants. He now risks being deported." Gallagher's words heated up the assembly. They gave him a standing ovation peppered with shouts of protest. At this point Jodoin called out Starr and demanded to know what he intended to do about this terrible situation. Starr was on the spot. He had no choice but to take a stand and so he publicly committed himself to preventing my deportation. Just like that, the threat was gone. A few years later, my criminal record was also erased.

I met Michael Starr when he became the chairman of the Ontario Workmen's Compensation Board and personally thanked him for having intervened in my favour.

CHAPTER 7

STREET CRED

I got out of jail in 1962 and went straight back to my job as an organizer. Now, of course, I enjoyed a certain respectability, given my trials and tribulations. I had what they call street cred. In the British trade union movement, going to prison during a strike is a badge of honour and, similarly, in Canada my jail time had made me famous in the movement.

Something else of great importance to me happened that spring. An Italian parish priest named Giuseppe Carraro had founded an organization called COSTI (Centro Organizzativo Scuole Tecniche Italiane) to help Italian immigrants. Carraro asked a number of organizations for financial help, Local 183 included. On Gallagher's recommendation, we responded with a donation of $1,000, the only union to do so. I delivered the cheque to the COSTI office. At the time, it was a substantial donation; the average annual family wage was about $6,000. I took the funds to the tiny COSTI offices on Dundas Street West at Lansdowne Road in front of St. Helen's church. It was a fateful visit because it is where I met Rita, the woman I would marry.

We did not get off to a promising start. She kept turning down my requests to take her out. Not only that, she tried every way she knew to discourage me. After I accepted Marino Toppan's request to be the godfather to his first-born, Maurizio, I asked Rita to join me at the baptism and be the godmother. Finally, she relented. As a good native of the Trentino region of Italy, it was an obligation she could not refuse.

COSTI soon became an important organization within the Italian community under the leadership of its first director, Carletto Caccia, a man of considerable capacities. He went on to become a municipal councillor, a Member of Parliament, and, finally, Minister of Labour in the federal government. He served under Prime Ministers Pierre Trudeau and John Turner. The talented Consul General of Italy back then, Dr. Cappetta, also helped the cause, organizing many events and even committing himself beyond his political mandate, just to help the Toronto Italian community. The COSTI headquarters moved from Dundas to the present location of the Consulate General of Italy, 136 Beverley Street, in Toronto, at that time known as the Casa d'Italia (House of Italy). The Casa d'Italia was built by Italian immigrants before the Second World War and confiscated by the Canadian government during the conflict. It was released by the Canadian government but not to the Italian community in Canada. It was given instead to the Italian government. The building was in poor shape. At one point, it had been converted into stables for the Royal Canadian Mounted Police horses. I remember going to see Rita there and she was wearing a coat because it was so cold inside that building. COSTI refurbished the premises through the efforts of the workers who attended its training courses. They did such a good job repairing and renovating it that the Italian government claimed it back and COSTI had to find a new location. Today COSTI is still an important immigrant organization, catering to all newcomers.

It was not just the technical trades who were getting an education at the time. I was about to hit the books myself. In the summer of 1963, the Canadian Labour Congress launched a seven-week course for trade unionists at the University of Montreal. I asked Gallagher if I could attend and, as a far-sighted man, he agreed. Before being admitted to the labour college, I had to present a paper explaining why I wanted to attend. My English was not perfect and I needed help with editing and so where else should I turn but to Frank Drea, the *Telegram*'s labour reporter who had shed light on the plight of immigrant workers with his hard-hitting stories. He helped me out.

The labour college was of great benefit. I studied the history of trade unions in Canada and the country's political, economic, and social structure. There were many conferences at the college at which renowned leaders would give speeches. One in particular impressed me, delivered by René Lévesque, at that time Minister of Labour in the Liberal Government of Quebec but formerly a well-known journalist who had covered many big labour stories for the CBC. He had just started his career as an elected Member of the National Assembly, taking his seat in 1960.

During my time at the University of Montreal, I got to know other Canadian trade unionists taking the course, among them, Ray Ford of Labourers Local Union 506, who later became its business manager, and Keely Cumming, president of the CUPE Local Union 1000 (Canadian Union of Public Employees) which represented Ontario Hydro employees. I remember driving on Highway 401 to Montreal with Ford on June 1, 1963. It was about 6 a.m. and suddenly I broke out laughing. He asked me what was so funny. "I just remembered, today is June 1," I said, "and exactly two years ago today about this time I was arrested. Today, I'm going to the labour college in Montreal."

Cumming was a tall man, with blue eyes, blond hair, and a smile that would always put you in a good mood. He had served in the Canadian mercantile navy during the war and he told me about his part in a big brawl in Halifax at its end. VE (Victory in Europe) Day was a disaster in Halifax from the get-go. Everyone knew the war was ending and so when the announcement came on Monday, May 7, 1945, everything shut down so that civilians could celebrate for a couple of days. As Cumming told it, Halifax authorities closed all the bars for fear of drunken sailors celebrating and rioting. The sailors got so angry they kicked in the windows of the closed bars and turned the town upside down. A small-scale civil war broke out and went on for the better part of two days. Only the intervention of the army managed to calm things down. Cumming was a jovial person and a hard worker but, like his comrades in arms, he wanted his moment of fun.

We became good friends and we ended up talking a lot about the Canadian trade union movement, Canadian politics, and especially left-wing politics. He helped me expand my knowledge of these subjects at a time when the movement was gaining traction and growing quickly. We were no longer a bunch of malcontent immigrants. We were a real social movement with numbers, drawing members from all nationalities across the country.

This meant that Local 183 was getting busier and expanding. In 1962, we moved from the three small rooms on Bond Street over to Queen and McCaul on the second floor of a small building. The new headquarters was bigger and each one of us could have our own modest office. On the second floor were the small Lathers Union offices. The manager, who was Canadian-born, Ken Weller, was also arrested during the 1961 strike for obstructing police. He bragged that he had told the police officer to "Fuck off" but in court his charge was dismissed while another striker, a German arrested for obstructing police during the same strike, got a week's suspended sentence. With the same charge, during the same strike, I got six months.

Working with Weller was Gus Simone, who later became the head of that Local. Simone and I became good friends and we helped each other out. He was a dynamic young man with far-sighted views. Bit by bit, he managed to build up a powerful local. Gus always respected our friendship even when there were major differences between our locals. At the end of the corridor on the same floor was the Toronto Building and Construction Trades Council office, headed by business manager Albert Hall and his assistant Jack Greely.

From 1962 to 1963 I continued to work as a trade union organizer providing services to our members and slowly increasing our local membership. It was a meticulous and systematic job. By day I worked to resolve our members' problems and by night I went out to sign up new members and get their units certified at the Ontario Labour Relations Board. And so it went for the next few years. What had started as a struggle had become a routine job. That feeling would not last.

CHAPTER 8

THE EXPANSION
OF LOCAL 183

By 1964 things were changing all around us, both on the personal and working side. For one, I married my beautiful bride, Rita. I guess my persistence paid off. We had courted from 1962 and we married on January 6, 1964, at St Helen's at St. Clair West and Lansdowne Road. Unlike most Italian weddings, ours was small with only seventeen guests at our luncheon—again something different because most Italians celebrate a wedding with dinner. Why? I guess I just wanted to do something different. We were married on a Monday rather than the usual Saturday and we had to obtain special religious dispensation for that, since January 6 was also the Feast of the Epiphany, which the Vatican decrees a holiday.

For our honeymoon we went to Montreal in the dead of winter. On reflection, it was not the most exotic of choices but at the time, before the dawn of cheap commercial airfares, we did not think so much about going south or traveling to international locations. Niagara Falls and Montreal were prime destinations and we stayed at the very upscale Queen Elizabeth Hotel. After a few days, we took the train to North Bay to visit my sister and my brother. When we arrived the forests looked like something out of *Dr. Zhivago*. They were coated in ice and glistened like diamonds in the moonlight. Unfortunately, it was also something like minus-forty degrees Celsius and the seats in my brother-in-law's car were frozen. It felt like we were sitting on rocks. After a few days there we went back to Toronto and I went back to the trenches, literally. I was organizing non-union contractors in the sewer and water-main sector.

Local 183 was representing about half of the sewer and water-main industry but our collective agreement had expired at the end of November 1963. At that time, we were part of the Council of Trade Unions formed by the Operating Engineers Local 793, the Teamsters Local 230 and ourselves. The chairman of the council was the business manager of the Operating Engineers, Herb Ingram, a tough no-nonsense trade unionist. Ingram, like most leaders of his local, came from the Toronto coal docks, an industry which was one of the first organized by his union.

Ingram called the shots in the administration of the Council of Trade Unions, especially during negotiations with employers. For some strange reason he decided to call a strike toward the end of February 1964 during a harsh winter. Why he called the strike at that time is still a mystery to me. It is no fun being on a picket line in a Toronto winter and getting anywhere to head off strike-breakers or move pickets is a nightmare. Anyway, Gallagher was sick in hospital, Reilly was about to leave for Harvard University to attend a trade union course sponsored by our International, and I was just twenty-three years old. Who would listen to me?

Before leaving, Reilly told me to call a meeting and tell the members we were on strike. It all sounded very simple. The problem was that there was no time. I decided to print a number of pamphlets in English and Italian and nail them on job sites informing the members that as of the following Monday we were on a legal strike and instructing them to report to the union office that day at 7 a.m.

Most of our newly organized members had never been on strike before. They were of different nationalities, new to Canada. In the tunnel sector, they were mostly Slavic and Polish and I had no idea how many would show up. To my surprise, it was a complete success. It was another important lesson. It taught me to have faith in workers' solidarity, a principle which has guided me during all my trade union activities. The biggest problem during the strike was the non-union contractors who kept working. To Canadian members, who were primarily in the Operating Engineers Union, this was no problem but the Italian workers could not understand it. They believed a strike is a strike and nobody should be working.

A strike is not for the faint of heart and it dragged on for two months, into the middle of April, when a conciliation officer appointed by the Minister of Labour called a morning meeting of the parties at the King Edward Hotel. There were committees from the various unions and from the employers who were represented by the very able lawyer Stanley Dinsdale. I clearly remember remarks made to me at the start of the meeting, by the president of the Operating Engineers Local 793, Joe McClory, an elderly, old-school union man, tall and rather bony:

Look at all the committees present here and the lawyers. Everything must be recorded and voted in secret vote by the members! In my days we used to do things on a handshake. We would meet with a couple of representatives from the Toronto Construction Association at the northeast corner of Church Street and Queen Street East and, after a brief discussion, we would agree if there was going to be an increase (usually a few cents) or not. We shook hands and that was it. No big fancy lunch and expensive wine, not even a cup of coffee. There was mutual respect and both parties lived up to the deal. We reported back to the members who accepted the deal.

That was the best we could do. No vote was needed. They had full confidence in us.

Ingram, who had called the strike, wanted a free hand to deal with the employers without involving the rest of us. The collective agreement consisted of three sections: a master portion and two schedules. Schedule A dealt with open-cut construction, and Schedule B the tunnel work. Each schedule listed every union job classification, hourly rates, hours of work, and the premium rates for working with compressed air. In a construction collective agreement job classifications are very important. They give a union the right to represent the workers performing those skills as well to establish premium rates for skilled workers rather than lumping everyone together as non-specific labourers.

Ingram, handling the master portion and Schedule A, asked me to deal with Schedule B, considered at that time a small part of the sector. I found myself sitting across from Garth Jenkins, an engineer from McNally and Sons, a sincere and straight-talking man. I was assisted by Jack Dillon, who had been hired by Gallagher from his hospital bed. Dillon was an old miner working in the subway. He was a good man, a little bit rough, with a language all his own. The first thing he said to me after reviewing the sewer and water-main tunnel schedule was: "This is no fucking good. There are not enough job classifications in this schedule. There is only the classification of muckers [an assistant miner]."

I knew nothing about tunnel work so I asked Jack to explain it and the two of us approached Jenkins and asked for the inclusion of a number of job classifications with an appropriate premium pay to reflect the skills needed for them. Among these were the classifications of miner, lead miner, tunnel shield, and mole driver. Jenkins agreed. I had no idea of the fire I was about to light.

At around 3 a.m., I was told to suspend my negotiation because Ingram had reached an overall increase of 35 cents more over three years. Not much today but not bad then. Ten minutes later, Herb was screaming blue murder and the understanding was off. He had just discovered what I had done in adding the classifications.

He had cause to be upset. Those new jobs classifications should probably have been included under the Operating Engineers group, not under the Labourers classifications.

Of course, Ingram was furious because he saw me and Local 183 as encroaching on his territory and poaching members to our side. He considered such jobs as mole driver (more formally called the mole machine operator) as part of his union's jurisdiction.

We were all speechless, all except Ingram. Everything was going to blow up in our faces. At that point, the employers' lawyer, Dinsdale, proposed a compromise: leave things as they were and let the two International Unions in Washington decide which job classifications went to what union. We accepted the suggestion and moved on.

Oddly, Ingram never followed up with Washington. It is odd because I think he would have won the case. Across North America, the work in question had always been done by his members. In any event, Local 183 now represented all underground employees from the collar of the shaft down, including operators of sophisticated equipment. This was a turning point and the beginning of Local 183's expansion from a common labourer local to what it is today, representing a diverse number of trades.

It was also another valuable lesson for me. I learned the importance of job classifications in collective agreements and from that day forward I used it as a strategy, day in and day out. Unions fight hard to add members. Each new member adds more clout to the local. Each new member brings in more dues and adds more money to the pension fund. Big, well-financed locals are able to take stronger bargaining positions because if they strike, they can shut down entire projects indefinitely since their members perform so many jobs on that site. It also means their strike funds are more robust, although I always refused to have a strike fund because, as Gallagher told me, they just prolong strikes. Ultimately, of course, strong unions win better working conditions and collective agreements for their members, and that is the real goal.

While the goal is to grow, there are times when an opportunity to represent a trade already covered by a collective agreement is best set aside to preserve the peace between unions. For example, about this time, I organized Armstrong Brothers, a Brampton civil engineering construction company. Armstrong Brothers was engaged primarily in roads, and sewer and water-main construction, employing about 150 workers. We applied for our usual bargaining unit as "all construction labourers," and we were certified as their bargaining agent by the Ontario Labour Relations Board as a matter of course. At the start of negotiation, much to my surprise, the company demanded that we represent all of their construction employees including the operating engineers.

Now, at that time we had a good relationship with the Operating Engineers Local 793. Their support would be essential during a strike so this was a sticky issue. We could not cross them. I came up with a proposal: "Let us sign on all construction employees under our agreement and in return we will forward the monthly dues for each operator to 793." At the end of the three-year agreement, Local 793 would then have been in a position to apply for certification of the bargaining unit. They had already tried a number of times to gain certification and had failed so this was a good plan and it was accepted. Every month we dutifully forwarded all dues on behalf of each operating engineer. Local 793 was so impressed by our diligence in this matter that they invited me to dinner along with our secretary who handled the remittances. I chose The 54 restaurant (later renamed Canoe) on the fifty-fourth floor of the TD Centre. Our host was Harvie Herron, a pleasant and dedicated union officer. Naturally, I ordered the very best, especially the wine. The cost was over $600, which at that time was a full month's salary. Some days later, Herron called me and asked if he could add a couple of other union officers' names to the bill because his executive was willing to pay but was having a hard time believing only three of us rang up a $600 bill. Fine with me.

Our relationship with Armstrong also brought us close to a conflict with another union, the Carpenters. In 1966, Armstrong was awarded the water reservoir project at Finch Avenue West and Dufferin Street. The job superintendent called our union office for a number of carpenters since the project required concrete walls and there was forming work to be done. At that time, we did not represent carpenters and I was concerned I would end up stepping on the toes of the Carpenters Union. Our collective agreement with the company, however, required us to represent all construction employees.

I consulted with Reilly who saw a golden opportunity to expand our jurisdiction. I referred to the project a number of manhole builders who in our opinion were good form setters because at that time manholes were built on the job, not prefabricated. A few days later, I inquired of the job superintendent how our "carpenters" were doing. He said: "They are not carpenters but they are good workers and form setters and in a short time I will train them to be good carpenters." And so we started to represent carpenters as a trade. With time, we came to represent more carpenters than the Carpenters Union in Toronto and I will come back to that later because it became a real issue and probably still will be long after I am gone.

The sun was shining on the construction sector in the mid-1960s. Toronto was booming from north to south and east to west. The population was growing, new residential subdivisions were spreading out, apartments were rising, and an ambitious new transportation plan was in place. Major projects like the Highway 401 expansion, the first and second phases of the W. R. Allen Expressway, Highway 427, and others were rolling out. Each required not only roads but also major structures such as bridges, retaining walls, culverts, and more. Technically, Local 183 did not have the so-called jurisdiction over this type of construction because structures were still under Local 506. However, our view was very simple: if it is not organized it is fair play, and we aggressively organized the heavy construction sector while Local 506 was asleep at the wheel. As the old saying goes, possession nine-tenths of the law. By the time Local 506 started to complain to the International Union it was too late. The International had no choice but to recognize the reality on the ground.

The incident with Armstrong Brothers taught us how to expand our jurisdiction and shortly afterward we had created the job classification of "form setter," which really meant "carpenter" in the heavy construction collective agreement. The contractors did not oppose us for two reasons: one, because in Local 183 there was a reserve of good productive workers who could easily adapt to this trade, particularly the Italian immigrants; and two, it meant the elimination of jurisdictional disputes between two unions which was important to contractors. For them, time is money, and quibbles over whose job or jurisdiction something is are time consuming, slowing down production and piling up legal bills. Within a few years, all carpentry work in all heavy construction jobs was performed by members of Local 183.

CHAPTER 9

THE SAFETY CRUSADE

After the Hogg's Hollow tragedy of 1960, the Ontario government enacted legislation to improve safety on construction sites. There were major improvements but still not enough was actually done. The fact is that construction sites are dangerous places. In January 2014, the *Globe and Mail* published a list of the ten most dangerous jobs. Many people think policing or being a firefighter is dangerous. Those jobs did not make the list. Logging and commercial fishing are numbers one and two while roofers ranked fourth, structural steel fifth, power line installation and repair seventh, and construction tenth. It has always been thus and that is why unions fight so hard for safety issues. It really is a matter of life and death.

To Gallagher, job safety was of paramount importance. He made it a personal crusade. Every time he considered a project unsafe he would shut it down, put members around it with signs declaring "Job Unsafe," and call the news media to get maximum exposure to the cause. He even hired a full-time safety representative, Norm Pike.

In the beginning Gallagher received a lot of news coverage for his cause but over time the interest faded. There were two problems with his campaign. First, there had been no real improvement in safety laws. Second, the shutdowns were expensive for the union because members doing picket duty for safety reasons were paid by the local. At the time, I was the secretary treasurer of the local. Our finances were so tight we often scrambled to meet payroll. Safety, however, was too important to abandon. I had to think of another way: to change the law. To achieve that, we needed the support of all major labour bodies. I decided to send a letter to the three major labour organizations, the Ontario Federation of Labour, the Provincial Building Trades Council, and the Toronto Building and Construction Trades Council, inviting them to a meeting at my small office to talk about safety. I did this because I remembered my conversations with Ed Boyer who told me if you want to change something, change the law.

To my surprise, all three labour federations demonstrated a strong interest in this vital issue and came to our meeting. This was a big kudo because I was still just a kid and it was like the mountains coming to Muhammad. Our plan was to change the law, so I thought we should have a lawyer. I asked Syd Robin and he sent along a young lawyer named Ray Koskie. A committee was established with representatives from all three labour organizations. A few months later, the committee came up with thirty recommendations. The two most important were the right of a worker to refuse to work in unsafe conditions and the authority of a safety inspector to stop the work if he or she deemed the job unsafe. Nowadays, these rights are considered of cardinal importance but in those days we were breaking new ground. The committee's recommendations were included in a brief that was presented to the Ontario government. Most of our recommendations were adopted into law. Gallagher's safety campaign and the publicity he generated were instrumental in this victory: his untiring efforts raised the profile of the issue and got the ball rolling. What he started saved many, many lives and we are beholden to him.

Safety remains a tricky issue on construction sites and it requires constant vigilance. Sometimes the problem is not lapses in standard practices but the standard practices themselves. Case in point, subway tunnels. In those days, most tunnels, including the subway tunnels, were excavated using a pressurized air system to prevent underground water from flooding the tunnels. This was the system being used at the Hogg's Hollow site but on larger projects they were much more sophisticated. At the entrance of each tunnel were heavy airlocks to contain air pressure up to fifty atmospheres. At the entrance, there was a chamber for compression and decompression purposes. Each miner had to undergo a process to prevent the bends, much like scuba divers do when they prepare to surface after breathing compressed air under water and dealing with the pressure of the ocean itself. Working with compressed air is a dangerous job if not regulated properly or if the rules are ignored. The problem back then was that there were no clear rules, partly because we knew nothing about the effects of working with compressed air for any length of time.

In fact, it took until 1969, when Dr. George Gamarra, doing his internship at Toronto East General Hospital, approached our local asking for funding to start a study for compressed air work. We agreed immediately. He placed rabbits at various atmospheric pressures and conducted a number of experiments on them with compression and decompression times. He then studied and dissected the rabbits' livers to determine the effect of the compressed air. The only similar studies that had been conducted before were those of various navies, in particular the U.S. Navy.

Here's how Liberal MPP D. M. DeMonte (Dovercourt) raised some of Dr. Gamarra's findings in the Ontario Legislature on February 25, 1969:

Dr. Gamarra of the East General Hospital, Mr. Speaker, who has specialized in de-compression sickness, says that a man can be exposed to compressed air for several months without showing any signs or symptoms. Then, in a moment, he might develop tell-tale signs of the illness: the pain in the joints, the itching skin, the difficulty in breathing and the tiredness, possibly even bleeding from the nose or ears. Furthermore, these symptoms might be delayed for as much as two years after a man leaves the tunnel. How, then, does a lay workman prove his case in the absence of back-up medical opinion in this new field?

This medical specialist is vociferous in his call for a complete set of X-rays before a man enters caisson work. Otherwise, there can be no basis for future comparison. The cause of new lesions cannot be pinned down. He says: "Hardly a man working under compressed air in Toronto has had previous X-rays. I don't recall anyone having been examined radiologically. This creates a problem, not only for the compensation board, but also for the worker, because there are several other factors which can resemble the same type of lesion."

Dr. Gamarra came up with a chart with precise time periods for compression, decompression, and time allowed to work under such conditions according to the atmospheric pressure being used—the higher the atmospheric pressure, the shorter the work shift and the longer the period for compression and decompression.

Our findings were presented to the Ontario Ministry of Labour. By coincidence, right at that time there was a front-page story which propelled our cause up the ladder. One of our tunnel workers had been arrested for what was thought to be drunk driving. However, his condition was not due to alcohol but to the bends. He was rushed by helicopter to a Buffalo hospital which had a hyperbaric chamber since none of the Toronto hospitals had one back then. His case got considerable coverage.

Our compression schedule became law. Ontario became a leader in tunnel safety and our union negotiated good bonuses and shorter hours for people working in those conditions. These premiums were substantial. Miners had to undergo a medical checkup before working in a compressed air tunnel and, on a subway project, a doctor was present at the moment of hiring. Over time, compressed air work was phased out as the technology changed. The new method was a system of sinking pipes before the work began to suck and pump out the water continuously. We lost the bonus but the better news was that the technology eliminated the danger of having to work in compressed air.

CHAPTER 10

THE STRIKE OF 1967

For some reason, in the spring of 1967, the Operating Engineers Local 793 withdrew from the Council of Trade Unions. The Council had been founded in 1959 by Local 793, Teamsters Local 230, and Local 183 to jointly negotiate for roads, and sewer and water-main construction, sectors which were represented by large contractors' associations. My guess was that Herb Ingram, business manager of 793, wanted a free hand to negotiate an agreement for his own local and that he considered the rest of us a burden. Ingram was able to reach a fair settlement for his union without a strike but we were not so fortunate.

The employers' proposals to us were far inferior to the contract signed by the Operating Engineers and it forced us to strike. We lined up against three contractors' associations: the Heavy Construction Association (Toronto), the Metropolitan Toronto Road and Builders Association, and the Metropolitan Toronto Sewer and Watermain Contractors Association. All three were represented by Stan Dinsdale, the astute management labour lawyer. The employers in each association were tough people, conservative and experienced fighters. This would be no easy battle.

The employers were not anti-union, just old-school. It was easier to pull a tooth from them than to get a few cents more an hour. They were convinced our demands were cooked up by the union and not reflective of what their employees were directing us to do. By settling with the Operating Engineers, they were trying to divide and weaken us. At that time, we represented a majority of their employees since the industry was not as mechanized as it is today. Just before the strike, Gallagher fell ill and was hospitalized. Being the secretary treasurer, the second-ranking position with the local, I had to take responsibility to direct the labour dispute. I was twenty-six years old. Reilly, of course, was of great assistance, as always, and we held weekly meetings at the Lansdowne Theatre and rented the basement of a church at Dundas and Keele for our strike headquarters.

Not wanting to repeat the mistakes of Irvine and Zanini, I did not use any flying squads but instead used just two members for picket duty at various job sites because the propensity for violence was too great and violence would bring bad publicity which would ultimately hurt our cause. You cannot force workers not to go to work unless they truly believe in the justness of a strike and willingly refuse to cross a picket line.

We were highly successful. Our members fought bravely. Most of them had just come off a long spell of winter unemployment and had big financial burdens and families to support. Many had been in Canada only a few years and most were Italian immigrants. I was in awe of their will to fight, knowing the financial conditions most were in.

As expected, it was a tough strike. We tried our best to help those members who desperately needed financial assistance, setting up a committee to evaluate the numerous requests for aid. We, the union officers, gave up our pay for the duration of the strike to help those in need and towards the end our finances also dried up. Still, we were always game for a laugh. I remember a contractor had a horse running at Woodbine Racetrack named

Hail Mary. He called us and said that his horse looked good. We understood that as an insider's tip and Reilly and I took a short break from our long days to go to the track to bet a few dollars. The horse won and paid well. When we got back, I called the contractor and told him that now we were in a position to carry on with the strike for a few more weeks because we had bet all the money left in the strike fund and made a killing on his horse.

The strike lasted for seven long weeks. It ended only after the employers were fully convinced that our proposals were from their employees and not a figment of our imaginations. Months later I found out that in the sixth week of the strike, the contractors sent some of their most trusted working foremen to our meetings. All of them reported back to each contractor the same story: the members were the ones who were making the wage demands and who wanted to fight on. After a long day-and-night negotiating session at the Ministry of Labour at 8 York Street we reached a tentative settlement. We got an 85-cent-an-hour increase each year for three years along with improvements in working conditions. Today, that may not look like a lot but in those days it was a fair settlement.

I will never forget the day the agreement was ratified. Many members broke down in tears. They took me on their shoulders and carried me in triumph around the Lansdowne Theatre. The strike of 1967 was an important milestone in the history of Local 183 because it was the first time we had fought alone and won. We gained the respect of our opposition, of the employers, and of other construction unions. We were coming of age.

CHAPTER 11

ETHNIC CONFLICTS AND A SHOTGUN MEETING

In unions, as in politics and life, things change. A neighbourhood may initially be settled by one group of people but as their needs and preferences change they move on to new neighbourhoods. In downtown Toronto, Spadina was initially a Jewish area, known as The Ward. By the 1970s and '80s, it had become largely Asian. It is the same in unions. The first immigrants to Canada were Scots and Irish and English and, later, we Italians arrived along with Poles, Portuguese, and many other nationalities.

For some time, there was ethnic tension within the local as the old guard adjusted to the arrival of the newer members. In our case, the tension was primarily between a small group of Italian members and some Irish members. The Italian group was led by Biaggio Di Giovanni, the patriarch of a large Italian family, all members of the local and good workers, although they were a minority among our Italian members. Their major complaint was that the best jobs were given to the Irish.

In those days the best jobs were in subway construction where hourly rates were higher and working conditions were better. Together with bridge building, it was the only sector of the local with a full hiring hall, which meant the employer had to call the union for his manpower instead of hiring off the street. Although the hiring hall system was well established with other building trade unions in the commercial sector, I was not in favour of it. My objection was simple. With a hiring hall system, members regarded the union as an employment agency and they blamed the union, rather than economic or political conditions, when they were out of work. My idea of a union was for members to regard it as the body representing workers in the quest for better working conditions and as a source for help with their problems on and off the job. In time, I was proven right. Most building trades unions either watered down or got rid of the hiring halls, although some trades still use the system or a variation of it today.

Di Giovanni's complaint was not without merit but there were good reasons why the Irish were predominantly working in subway construction. It was difficult for the Irish to work on other construction sections where the overwhelming majority were either Italian or Portuguese. It was not a case of discrimination. It was a question of language and practice. On those projects the working language was Italian and the methods were different. For an Irishman, it was like being a fish out of water. I also knew the few hundred Irishmen we represented were loyal to our union and ready to fight anytime I called upon them.

In the spring of 1968, Di Giovanni brought his complaints to the Italian-language newspaper *Corriere Canadese*. At that time, it had just hired a director and an assistant both recently arrived from Rome and while they were experienced journalists and good at their jobs, they knew nothing of Canadian realities. Unfortunately, they published a series of articles in which Di Giovanni accused Gallagher of all kinds of skulduggery and wrongdoing. Gallagher was understandably upset. He laid charges against Di Giovanni under the union constitution. Di Giovanni was tried by the union trial board, found guilty, and suspended from the local. However, the trial board's finding, by the constitution rules, had to be approved by the members at the next monthly membership meeting before it could be implemented.

It was April 1968. The meeting was held at the Labor Lyceum on Spadina Avenue, now a Chinese shopping centre. At that time, all monthly meetings were held in the evenings. I later changed the time to Sunday morning to make it easier for members to attend. At this particular meeting, the hall was at capacity with more than five hundred members, split more or less evenly for and against Di Giovanni.

I was on the stage with Reilly, Gallagher, and Mike O'Brien, a full-time union representative. O'Brien, incidentally, became a good friend and visited my house many times to eat Italian food. He was well liked by the Irish because he was a nephew of Michael Collins, a hero of the Irish independence movement. As soon as the minutes of the trial board were read at the meeting, chairs started to fly. It was like a scene out of a movie. I did not know what to do. I noticed O'Brien jumping from a window next to the stage. I said to myself: "If it is good enough for the nephew of an Irish national hero, it is good enough for me." I followed O'Brien.

Shortly after the brawl started, all kinds of police officers arrived. They re-established order but the meeting was adjourned. The decision of the executive board, the only one ever made for expulsion of a member from the local union in my thirty-two years, was never implemented. Over time, under my leadership, the ethnic conflict died down and harmony prevailed between ethnic groups. The Di Giovanni family continued to be strong union supporters though there were other showdowns, as I will describe later.

* * *

Later that year, in October, there was a vacancy in the executive board of the local for the position of recording secretary, an unpaid position. The executive board meetings were held monthly on Saturday mornings because three of the members worked during the week. The executive board of the local consisted of seven members, the president (which was not a full-time position), the vice-president, the recording secretary, the secretary treasurer, the business manager (the most important position), and two other executive members. At that time, I was the secretary treasurer, the second-most important position.

On October 5, 1968, at about 10 a.m., we were sitting in the small boardroom on the second floor of the union office on St. Clair Avenue. Our constant organizing had increased our membership and we had outgrown the Queen and McCaul office. A couple of years earlier we had purchased a two-storey building with about 1,500 square feet of space on St. Clair West and that was where we were, waiting for Mike Reilly, who would act as the chairman. Reilly was the full-time business agent and he was busy downstairs taking care of some members' needs. Suddenly, Jim Gibb, one of our members, burst into the boardroom and pulled a brand-new shotgun from a cardboard box.

No one paid much attention to him. The last thing you are looking for is a member with a shotgun. Jim worked in subway construction and I knew him so, having spotted the gun, I got up slowly from my chair, walked over, and said: "Hey, that's a nice hunting gun you have, Jim." Jim pointed the gun at me, then rotated, pointing at the others around the table, in particular Gerry Gallagher. "Today you will appoint me to the position of recording secretary," he said.

We were all shocked but Gerry calmly responded: "We'd be happy to do it, Jimmy, but we can't start the meeting without the chairman."

"Where is he?"

"He's downstairs," said Gerry.

Jimmy pointed at me and yelled for me to go and get him.

I did not wait to be asked twice and gladly left the room to tell Reilly what was going on. Reilly asked me to call the police and bravely headed upstairs. Shortly after, an executive board member, Frank Palazzolo, rushed down and said not to call the police as per Jimmy's wishes. It was too late. The police had already been called but before they arrived I heard a commotion from the board room and went up to investigate. I found Jimmy on the floor, bleeding slightly from the head. Apparently, he had asked for a glass of water and Reilly was more than happy to comply. Wisely, though, he kept the glass at a distance from Jim, who, in order to grab it, took his finger off the trigger. As he did, Dan Ryan, another member of the executive board and full-time business agent, grabbed the gun from Jimmy who then got a whack over the head with the barrel.

The police arrived shortly after and arrested him. The surprise came later when Jim Gibb went to court. For such a serious offence he got off with a very light sentence. His lawyer put up a brilliant defence. He said Jim had been damaged by sad experiences with the Seafarers' International Union and Hal Banks, and that he had only pulled the gun in our offices in self-defence. Gallagher was very upset at the light sentence, as we all were, and rightly so.

CHAPTER 12

A CASE OF INDIGESTION

Shortly after the strike of 1967, I fell very ill with something which had been bothering me periodically for a year or more. From time to time, I would develop a high fever, start sweating profoundly, and my stomach and digestive system would rumble. There was no apparent explanation for it. I went to the hospital emergency room many times and my own doctor ran all kinds of tests and analyses and everything came back negative. He was convinced it was all in my head but it was very real to me.

It was a bad time to be sick. I had scheduled the start of construction on my first house on a lot I had bought from the Robert Home Smith Company. Robert Home Smith had been a major figure in Toronto's early history, from 1900 to about 1935. He had acquired some 3,000 acres of land in South Etobicoke, much of which he developed, selling lovely English-style homes to new immigrants from the United Kingdom. "A little bit of England in Canada," the advertising materials offered. My lot was on Allanhurst Drive south of Eglinton at Royal York Road. The morning they started the excavation, a hot August day, I was in bed shivering. Anxious about my first house, I asked Rita to go and see if they had started the job.

She came back crying. When I asked what was wrong she said she was overcome with emotion at seeing our house started. At that time, we were renting a small apartment and we were desperate to move up. That was it. I could not resist the temptation to go see for myself so I put on a heavy winter coat and asked her to drive me over. I knew I had to get better and be strong to go on with the next chapter of our lives together and, of course, to continue my work in building a union.

I do not remember all the circumstances but one day I went to see a Dr. McCrae in Forest Hill about my illness. After examining me, he said I was suffering from a virus infection and that there was no medicine to fight it. He knew this because he himself had experienced a similar condition. He also said that my immune system would be the only thing to fight the virus and he put me on a strict diet combined with a periodic shot of vitamins.

Doc McRae was no ordinary doctor. He had fought with the British Commandos in World War II and had participated in the raid to kill Marshal Erwin Rommel. He was one of the three commandos to escape and he later fought in Italy and came to know the Italians. He developed an appreciation for our culture and he often kept me in his study telling me his war stories. I survived that bout of illness and, as the good doctor predicted, my immune system overcame the virus after another year or so. Just like that, one morning I woke up and felt stronger so I celebrated with a whole bottle of wine and felt fine. The day before, just a few drops of wine would have made me sick. Strange how the body works.

Throughout 1968, we kept on organizing, providing services to our members and expanding our work jurisdictions to the 3,000-members mark. That same year, Zanini, the man who had fired me to hire a relative in 1960, was discharged from prison after serving a two-year sentence for break and enter. He always claimed to be innocent. His friend, Charlie Irvine, convinced Gus Simone of the Lathers Union Local 562 to hire Zanini to organize the residential concrete forming industry because there had been a boom in rental high-rise construction for several years.

The speed, ease, and economic efficiency with which these rental towers rose was due in part to a young Italian immigrant from the Abruzzi region, Nick Di Lorenzo, who with his two brothers, John and Fred, founded Di Lorenzo Construction, a concrete forming company and one of the biggest construction trade employers in Canada. Concrete forming is the process of taking "wet" concrete and pouring it into a mould or "form." The form is usually made from wood and creates a space for the concrete to flow into and then cure. You can make a form for paving a road just as you can make a form to create a wall or an apartment building. The Di Lorenzos hired Italian immigrants literally off the dock in Halifax or Montreal as they arrived, and put them to work making and filling forms.

The brothers introduced the so-called flying form concept to Toronto construction. A flying form is a mould which can be easily taken apart after the concrete sets and moved quickly to the next position for the next pour. It literally "flies" up the side of the building. The brothers also introduced the composite crew which greatly increased efficiencies and allowed a contractor to use tradesmen on the site to do whatever task was necessary. A carpenter would do labourers' work and vice versa. Rod installation was performed by employees of the forming contractor rather than by the rod man of the steel companies. This has an advantage in productivity because the forming contractor could schedule his own work rather than wait for the steel company installers. Composite crews were a no-no in commercial concrete forming construction because in that sector each union was responsible for its own work area and protective of its jurisdiction.

The Di Lorenzos, however, were doing non-union residential work. Their company's efficiencies allowed it to become the main contractor in the residential concrete forming sector in Ontario, employing at one point more than 1,500 workers. Not bad for three unskilled Italian immigrants.

Prior to 1968, the Carpenters, the Iron Workers, the Cement Masons, the Operating Engineers, and Labourers Local 506 had joined to create the Council of Concrete Forming Unions in an effort to organize companies such as Di Lorenzo. They were only modestly successful. Di Lorenzo was able to work non-union contracts because the company operated a number of subsidiaries and as soon as one was organized he would shut it down and start another. As noted earlier, the Ontario government intervened and amended the Ontario Labour Relations Act, Section 10.4, to make it more difficult for an employer to escape from certified union representation of its employees. Still, after some effort the Council of Concrete Forming Unions represented a small minority of the residential construction industry.

Against this background, Irvine, Zanini, and Simone, representing the Lathers Union, made a grand entrance. They pushed aside the Council of Concrete Forming Unions and offered contractors in the sector one union which meant no jurisdictional disputes and acceptance of the composite crew, together with very favourable wages and working conditions. In a short time, their collective agreement was signed by most residential concrete forming contractors. There was one problem, however. The big International Unions of carpenters, iron workers and labourers would not accept that their jurisdiction could be usurped by the smallest of them, the lathers. At that time, the Lathers International Union represented only 10,000 members in all of North America and Simone's local alone comprised about 15 per cent of that total. The big internationals, representing hundreds of thousands of workers, applied pressure through the Building and Construction Trades Department of the AFL-CIO in

Washington to have the Lathers give up the concrete forming in Toronto. It was quite a fight and it got ugly at times.

While this was all brewing, I had become the business manager of Local 183. This change happened suddenly. One day in the spring of 1969, Gallagher called me in and said: "I am quitting the office of business manager and want to be president of the local." After this big surprise he added another: "I want you to be the manager."

"Me? Are you sure?"

"Yes," he replied.

"Why not Reilly?" I asked. Reilly was ten years older than me. I was twenty-eight at the time.

"I don't trust him," said Gallagher.

I did not appreciate Gallagher's statement. Reilly was like an older brother to me and I respected and admired him. Gerry, however, was a good judge of character, and in the end he would be proven right.

My new position did not much change my daily routine. At that time, I was the secretary treasurer, which can be a cozy office job but not the way I did it. I spent my time doing what was in the best interests of our members: organizing, providing services to them on and off the job, negotiating—responsibilities that usually fell within the business manager's position. Gallagher, as it turned out, gave me his title but nothing more. He continued to enjoy the same salary and benefits as before and, I should add, our respect, until he died around Labour Day in 1976.

Reilly moved on to become the business manager of a new Ontario organization set up by the Labourers International to coordinate the activities of the province's Labourers locals.

Knowing that the big international unions were opposed to the lathers' role in the concrete forming industry, I approached Gus Simone in my new capacity as business manager of Local 183. I knew him well. I suggested he join our local. It made sense because we were surpassing the 3,000-members mark. Our local was respected by our International for our organizing skills and we represented more than labourers. We had added carpenters and cement finishers in the heavy construction sector. We were better suited than the lathers to represent the concrete forming sector and I knew they could not hold out much longer due to the pressure from the top. Simone was interested in my proposal. I called our International in Washington and told them of my understanding with Simone. They were very interested, and in the spring of 1969, a meeting was held in Chicago, attended by, among others, Peter Fosco, general president of our International; Sol Maso, general president of the Lathers International; Bob Connerton, our general counsel in Washington; Ray Koskie, our lawyer in Toronto; Nick Di Lorenzo, Gus Simone, myself, and a few others.

It was decided at that meeting that the lathers would formally renounce the right to represent the concrete forming workers in Toronto. Local 183 would hire Simone's three representatives, including Zanini, guaranteeing them jobs. Every worker would sign up with us so we could make an application for certification with the Ministry of Labour for each forming company. Local 183 also committed itself to representing all of the construction trades as requested by the employers who wanted to deal with only one trade union. With everyone in agreement, Simone told me that he would send Zanini to our office to start with us two days later. Two days went by and I waited for Zanini in vain. I called him.

"Bruno, why aren't you in our office?" I asked.

"Why should I be there?"

"You mean Simone did not tell you anything?"

"I don't know anything at all!" he said.

It was then that I understood a game was being played. The following Sunday, Simone held the last meeting of his members working in the concrete forming industry and announced that he would no longer represent them. Irvine and Zanini also participated in the assembly. Irvine climbed up onstage and thundered:

"This week in Chicago they sold you off like cattle." Chicago was famous at the time for its slaughterhouses. It was a clear invitation for the members to break away from the International and become an autonomous Canadian trade union. "Go Canadian, boys," they shouted, and a new union was formed with Zanini at its head. Contractors were offered a new contract granting them favourable terms at the expense of the workers. I conveyed everything to our lawyer in Washington, Bob Connerton, who was surprised by Irvine's power. It was incredible to think that a vice-president of an International would think that he could go rogue without personal repercussions.

Obviously, the creation of an independent Canadian union was a threat to all the internationals and their affiliated locals on this side of the border. The Toronto Building and Construction Trades Council, representing a large number of affiliated locals of the international unions, held a series of special meetings to discuss the problem and how to fight back against the new Canadian organization. Meetings were also held with the apartment builders but these went nowhere. The builders' position was simple: this was none of their business; it was a dispute between unions. The Building and Construction Trades Council, led by two great unionists, Alex Main and Clive Ballantine, decided its best option was to close down all building sites where the new Canadian union members were working.

This was not easy. The locals represented by the Trades Council did not have a strong presence at most apartment construction sites because most of the contractors were non-union. They needed the full support of the Teamsters Union to halt concrete deliveries to the sites. Without concrete, everything in construction grinds to a halt. The Teamsters International sent a special representative from Chicago, Tony Capone, to help the Trades Council with its plan. Tony was an elderly gentleman, tall, bald, with a short neck. He was a distant relative of the famous Al, but a good man.

The strike started in the third week of August 1969, and it was a bitter one, with frequent confrontations on the job sites by the opposing unions. Both Alex and Clive worked tirelessly. Alex emphasized time and time again that the council would not tolerate this independent union. I worked closely with him, and a few times he came after-hours to my house to develop strategy. That was my introduction to the realities of the high-rise residential sector.

Sadly, one evening during the strike, I went home, parked my car in the garage, and went into the house to see Rita and our first baby, a son, Mark, who had been born July 4 that year. As I looked out the window, I noticed a car with four robust-looking men parked in front of my driveway. My first instinct was to protect my family so I got my hunting gun, loaded it, and called a police officer from the labour squad. At that time a special joint forces unit consisting of the Royal Canadian Mounted Police, Ontario Provincial Police, and what was then the Metro Toronto Police Force had been formed to deal with the violence and numerous acts of vandalism in the construction industry.

Two police cruises arrived at my residence. The car with the four strangers sped away just before the officers pulled up and found me at the front door with my gun. The officers grabbed my weapon and unloaded it, and asked me a few questions. I was so ramped up on my own adrenaline that when they gave me the gun back, I reloaded as they watched. They left without saying anything.

Both the builders and the concrete companies went to the Ontario Labour Relations Board with a cease-and-desist motion. The board declared the strike illegal and issued a back-to-work order. It is a serious offence with severe repercussions to ignore such an order. The Trades Council held a special meeting at which the Teamsters International representative said he had no alternative but to order his concrete drivers back to work. It was a complete defeat. We had made the mistake of using the Irvine-Zanini method, working outside the law.

We licked our wounds and decided on a new strategy to fight the new Canadian union. I joined the Council of Concrete Forming Unions and moved it into the Local 183 office. With encouragement from our International, we beefed it up with full-time organizers and began to compete with the new union the legal way.

CHAPTER 13

SUDBURY SATURDAY NIGHT

Local 183 was gaining a reputation as a strong union with a dedicated membership when, in the spring of 1968, we got a call from Bill Milner, the business manager of the Labourers Local 168 in Vancouver. Milner was an extraordinary man. Originally from Sudbury, he had moved to Vancouver where he became active in the labour movement and was elected to the top position of Local 168, representing tunnel and rock workers. When his International imposed the Canadian Pipeline collective agreement that it had negotiated on its Canadian locals, who had to service the contract, Milner pushed back. He objected to the agreement because it was binding coast-to-coast in Canada yet it contained rates far below those he had established in British Columbia. He was charged and suspended by his International for two years. His members respected him so much, though, that when his suspension was over they re-elected him to the local's top position.

Over the years, Local 183 had developed a strong friendship with a number of business managers across Canada and in particular with Milner and a Newfoundland local because we were the three labourers' locals representing underground workers. On that day in the spring of 1968, Milner was calling to tell us that a number of former members of his local were working in Sudbury for a non-union mining development contractor and wanted to be organized. There were approximately seven hundred miners working for Dravo, an American company, which, in turn, was subcontracting work from Inco, the International Nickle Company, then the largest nickel miner in the world and today owned by Vale of Brazil. Milner thought that ours was the appropriate local to represent the workers even though our International already had Local 493 in Sudbury.

Mike Reilly jumped at the opportunity. He went to Sudbury, contacted the people as directed by Milner, and formed an organizing committee. Within a few months we applied for certification. Despite the company's strong opposition, we were successful in our application at the Ontario Labour Relations Board. A process of hard bargaining took place but finally a collective agreement was reached. We opened an office in Sudbury and hired a full-time representative, Hugh MacDonald, and a secretary.

By this point in early 1969, I was the manager of Local 183 and it was my duty and responsibility to represent the Sudbury miners. Of course, I knew little about mining, being a city boy. The majority of the miners were from Eastern Canada and Finland. In the beginning, they looked at me suspiciously. I did not blame them. I was an Italian immigrant with no tunnel work experience and, really, not much in the way of construction experience, either. My work world was administration, making phone calls, going to meetings, organizing meetings, getting people to sign up, and running around taking care of members' concerns.

Gradually, I gained their trust, primarily because I was able to make major improvements in their collective agreement at renewal. Despite opposition from the United Steelworkers of America, representing many thousands of Inco employers, we expanded our operation and hired an additional representative, Steve McLelland. Under the new collective agreement, we established a benefits plan for things like sick pay, coverage of prescription drugs, and life insurance. The plan was administered by our local. To better serve the members, the Sudbury office secretary, Anne Morrison, was authorized to sign and issue the cheques for claims.

Part of my job was to make regular visits to our Sudbury office. One late evening I arrived tired after a long drive from Toronto and decided to go to bed early. At about 10 p.m. the phone rang. It was Anne Morrison inviting me for a drink downstairs. She had a friend with her by the name of Heidi. I begged off, saying I was bushed but she would have none of it. She insisted and I felt obliged to accept her invitation. I was staying at the Holiday Inn. On the ground floor there was a pub called Dangerous Dan Saloon and it was full of miners, hundreds of them.

When I got there it was crowded and most of the miners were fairly drunk. There were only a dozen women in the place, two of them sitting at my table, and it started to get ugly with guys coming up and hitting on the ladies. At one point, I had to stand up and take some men to task because the vulgarity was out of hand. I was afraid. I knew it would not take much to start a fight and have the whole place explode with flying chairs and bottles like in a Hollywood movie.

I insisted we should leave, saying I was tired and things were getting rough. Still, the ladies wanted to stay. I guess Stompin' Tom, the famous Canadian country singer knew what he was talking about in that song of his, "Sudbury Saturday Night." As the night wore on, Morrison invited me to spend the weekend with her in Sudbury. It was Thursday night and I had to think fast because I was a married man. I agreed, on condition that I be allowed to leave at that moment and get some sleep. I was up early the next morning and thinking how to get out of the commitment. I called my secretary in Toronto and asked her to call the Sudbury office looking for me. She was supposed to leave a message with Morrison saying I was wanted in North Bay Saturday morning because there was a major problem on a big project.

Now, it so happened that the Armstrong Brothers had a major heavy project in North Bay so this was partially true. I also told my assistant in Toronto I would call her back when I was in the Sudbury office and say I could not possibly get to North Bay because I was tied up with the local's business. The plan was that she would then call me back and say that the company's labour relations representative, Dan Fryszuck, had already left Brampton for North Bay and she was unable to reach him. Of course, in those days there were no cell phones so everything went as planned. I told Morrison "duty first" and escaped.

Sadly, within a year I had to fire Morrison. Our welfare plan was almost bankrupt and after an investigation we found out that she had been lax with claims. During layoffs, for example, there was a surge of sick pay claims. Of course, we all support the members and their needs but drawing sick pay during layoffs was hurting other members who were also paying into the plan. Morrison's problem was that she wanted to be popular with the members and she sure succeeded there. The day after her firing there were pickets in front of our office. In Toronto, I received a number of phone calls on her behalf. One of them was from the chancellor of Laurentian University. The first thing I said was: "You are calling for Anne Morrison, right?"

"How do you know?"

"Because the next call I am expecting on her behalf will be from the Pope."

He laughed and asked me to do the best I could. Elie Martel, the NDP MPP for Sudbury, also called; he invited me to his suite that night at the Royal York Hotel. I knew Elie well. He was a very good person. Privately, he agreed with me regarding the reason for termination but asked for a political compromise. We agreed to take Morrison back but took away her authority for the benefits plan, on condition she start looking for another job. Everything worked out as agreed. Later, I was told Morrison had moved to Ottawa and, being a bright person and knowing how to move within political circles, she made major strides in her career.

* * *

Another of my great memories of that Sudbury adventure involved Gallagher dropping by to talk with some miners in a bar and discovering that they thought some of Dravo's operations were unsafe. The next day he closed down all Dravo operations and took a committee to management with a list of safety deficiencies. Dravo agreed to many of them but not all, claiming the mine safety inspectors had cleared those items. Gallagher dug in and continued the strike which was a problem because Dravo was a multinational company and did not take kindly to being pushed around by a local union. It launched legal action against Gallagher and the local. It meant we might have to back off the strike and incur substantial legal costs. I knew things had gotten out of hand and that, by coincidence, that week the secretary treasurer of our International was in Toronto.

Verne Reid was a wonderful and humane man. In the course of talking to him about other issues, I explained the Dravo situation and said I would have to rush up to Sudbury to sort things out. Reid immediately offered to help. It turned out he knew one of the top executives at Dravo in the U.S. and would personally reach out to him. To smooth things politically with Gallagher, I suggested Reid send a telegram—that is how things were done back before text messaging and email—stating that he was fully aware that safety was a prime issue and that he would make it his priority on returning to the U.S.

Gallagher read the telegram to the striking miners and recommended that they return to work since the International had stepped up on their behalf and would have a high-level discussion. It was an out for him and gave him an exit with dignity. I never told him that I had arranged the whole thing.

Not long after, Verne Reid died and I went to his funeral in Tacoma, Washington, where I met Bob Connerton, the general counsel for the International union. We were at the funeral parlour and it was time to pay our respects yet Bob called me into a side room, wanting to talk business.

"Bob," I said. "I came here to pay my last respects, not to talk business."

With that, I left. To me, it's about people first.

Mining, like construction, is often boom or bust. With new nickel mining operations starting up around the world, Sudbury nickel mining began to decrease in importance. Inco laid off a number of employees and the United Steelworkers of America negotiated a non-subcontracting-out clause in the next collective agreement. The upshot was our membership was reduced to less than two hundred people, which was not enough to sustain an office and full-time staff. We reached an agreement with the International to transfer our members to the Sudbury local.

This kind of thing, being driven by external forces, never sits well with the membership and it was soon clear the members were not happy in the new local. A small delegation came to visit me in my house in Toronto twice to petition for a return of Local 183 but there was nothing I could do. Still, it was an honour and privilege to have represented such a militant and hard-working group of Canadians as those miners. Looking back on my career, I still consider it one of my greatest achievements to have represented and served them.

CHAPTER 14

A PROPHECY COME TRUE

At about the same time as we were dealing with our showdown with Zanini, big trouble broke out in a subway construction project. Robert McAlpine, the British company awarded the construction of two tunnels known as Y1 and Y2 on Yonge Street north of Eglinton Avenue, locked us out of one of the two projects.

The dispute was over bonus pay. After meeting certain milestones, our miners would receive bonuses, usually on a per-foot basis. It was typical behavior for the men to take their time before they were in the bonus and then, once those milestones were met, to start working like hell. McAlpine, unhappy with the progress being made in the early days of these projects, shut down one of the tunnels. I retaliated by closing down the other tunnel, hoping to bring the issue to a quick resolution. I called a special meeting of the miners at the Maple Leaf Ballroom on St. Clair Avenue, not far from our office, to explain the situation.

That morning as I was about to leave the office to go to the meeting I found the doors to our offices blocked by a group of about fifty Italian members of Local 183 led by Biaggio Di Giovanni and Ermenegildo Di Giacomo. They had pushed in and occupied the offices and they stopped anyone from calling the police. They told us that they intended to take over the local because it was high time it was run only by Italians. This, of course, was a familiar theme with the Di Giovanni family. I shrugged and explained that I had to leave to address the miners who were waiting for me and, out of respect, they let me go.

Waiting for me at the Maple Leaf Ballroom were about 150 miners. I started my speech not by addressing the labour dispute itself but by appealing to them on an emotional level. I do not remember exactly what I said but it was something like this: "My brothers, we came to this country from many distant lands. We came here for a better future for ourselves and for our families. This union will make it possible to achieve our dreams. Our strength is in our unity."

I went on to explain why I was late and detailed the occupation of our office. As I spoke, the room began to empty. The miners rushed to their cars and drove to the office where, apparently, the contingent occupying the offices melted away at the sight of the arriving miners. Many of the miners remained at the office all day to make sure we were protected.

McAlpine applied to the Ontario Labour Relations Board for a cease-and-desist order against our illegal strike and we went after their illegal lockout. The Board quite humorously said both of us were right and wrong, and more or less invited us to use common sense. We sat down and within a day reached an agreement on the bonus schedule, which was ratified by the miners.

The problems with Di Giovanni and Di Giacomo were smoothed over. They were good union members who had been manipulated by some militant individuals in the Italian community. The difference between their position and mine was simple. I am proud of my Italian roots but the Italian immigrants are much like other immigrant workers. They do not always speak the language or understand the labour laws and that is where their union can help them. It does not matter whether they are Portuguese, Spanish, or Italian. As much as possible, we worked with them in their own languages. Others took the view that they had to build up the Italian community at the expense of other immigrant communities. I believe that this attitude was encouraged by the federal government's multiculturalism policies which made all immigrant communities sensitive to their own interests rather than sensitive to the good of the whole. The government separated communities into voting blocs and triggered struggles for control within them. I found this approach divisive and unhelpful. I fought to keep Local 183 unified and working for all of its members, and won. I still feel that multiculturalism is frequently misinterpreted and exploited for political gain. No matter whether we are Canadian-Italians, or Canadian-Chinese, the Canadian aspect should come first. A mosaic works only when the underlying glue is strong. Ask the Romans. Their mosaics are still there for all to see.

It was a few days after all this excitement, on a marvellous first day of fall, September 21, 1969, that we were to baptize our first son, Mark, who had been born on the Fourth of July, an auspicious day for our American friends. We had invited about forty relatives and friends to our home to celebrate the happy occasion but that morning I woke up sick with what felt like a huge pressure in my chest. I was having a hard time breathing. I told my wife to go to church for the baptism and that I would catch up with everyone later. Meanwhile, my brother-in-law took me to the emergency wing of Toronto General Hospital. The doctors wanted to keep me under observation for a few days. They thought I might be having a heart attack. I told them that they were crazy. I was twenty-eight years old. In any event, I could not stay in hospital because forty people were waiting for me at home. All the more reason to stay in the hospital, they said.

Reluctantly, I agreed, provided that I had a private room. They kept me under observation for three days before they released me. It was not a heart attack but my chest muscles had tensed and locked, making it difficult for me to breathe.

During my brief spell in hospital, the miners from the two tunnels sent me a get-well card, signed by all of them and I even got one signed by the leaders of our International union, personally delivered to me by Reilly, who had just come back from Washington. Never doubt that those flowers and letters you send to people in hospital are truly appreciated and remembered.

All of this served to make me realize that I needed to learn to deal with the enormous stress my daily work entailed. I remembered a principle learned from a book I had read in Rome on Raya Yoga: you cannot tell your brain to stop thinking about something but you can distract it by thinking of something else. From then on, every evening before falling asleep, I would distract myself from problems big or small, real or imagined, by fantasizing about winning the lottery, or about military tactics. I was always fond of history, in particular why battles were won or lost. I would think about all the moves in a battle, until I fell into a deep sleep. When I woke in the morning, I was refreshed and ready again to take on any problems.

* * *

And it was a good thing, too, that I learned to deal with stress because with all this happening and a new baby at home, I went back to work to find another battle looming. After the disastrous 1969 strike by the Toronto Building and Construction Trades Council, we had decided to renew our efforts to fight Zanini's independent Canadian union in the concrete forming sector by revitalizing the Council of Concrete Forming Unions which I had just joined. New organizers were hired and a group coordinator was appointed, Tony Michaels from the Iron Workers Local 721.

Michael was a dedicated and experienced union representative but he was from a craft union not familiar with the composite crew concept or with the Italian mentality which prevailed in the workforce and among the employers. Three of the five full-time organizers came from our rank and file and from subway construction. They were Italian miners with little understanding of high-rise forming but they knew a lot about union militancy. Another, Chester De Toni came from the Marble, Terrazzo, and Tile Helper Local.

Most of the expenses of the Council of Concrete Forming Unions were borne by Local 183, although we could hardly afford it and we were forced to make a number of sacrifices by cutting other union activities. Despite this, we were always out-voted by the other four member unions at the council's regular meetings. The only one to support our cause from time to time was Frank Giles, president of the Operating Engineers 793.

My participation was initially slight for a number of reasons. First, our limited ability to manage the affairs of the Council of Concrete Forming Unions due to this voting structure and, second, my many duties and responsibilities to Local 183, including the Sudbury branch, as I have already explained. Additionally, all union collective agreements were being renewed in 1970, a process that occupied most of my time for half the year. By the fall of 1970, not seeing any progress in the council's efforts to organize concrete forming—Zanini still had the lion's share—I decided to do something about it.

I called our organizers working for the council to an off-the-record meeting and asked them the reason for our lack of progress. To my surprise, I was told that the workers did not trust the council. The few forming contractors that had agreements with our council, representing about 15 per cent of the industry, were not living up to the collective agreement. They were paying lower wages in comparison to Zanini's collective agreement, a violation of the council's collective agreement.

Shocked, I drafted a request for information regarding the project locations, building permits, names of builders, names of forming contactors, names of employees and their classifications, their paid hours of work, and the amounts that they should have been paid. This was quickly collected from our few projects. My plan was to apply a construction lien against any project not living up to the collective agreement, claiming the amounts that had been withheld from our workers. A regular grievance procedure would take too long. A lien would put the financing of the projects, and therefore the cash flows, on hold until the dispute was settled.

The other unions involved in the council prevented me from going forward. I was told that the contractors had been given the green light to pay whatever was necessary to compete against Zanini-organized contractors. In their opinion, this was the only way to fight the new independent union. Again, I was stunned.

In early 1971, I gave the council an ultimatum: give Local 183 full administrative control of the council with the right to organize, negotiate, and police the sector, or we would pull out and organize every worker into Local 183. If they gave us control we would commit to sending to each respective union its share of the monthly dues we received. They laughed at us. In their opinion, a local without much experience in building construction, with a young manager, could not succeed where they had already tried for many years and failed.

Still, Alex Main, the full-time manager of the Toronto Building and Construction Trades Council, understood my proposal was the only way out of the mess. He called a special meeting in the spring of 1971 at the Simcoe Hotel's Admiral Room and made an emotional appeal to the other unions to let me try. He almost begged them, saying it was the only solution for unity and the only way to stop Zanini's independent union. This time the other unions did not laugh but they still turned down Alex's appeal, albeit politely.

Our next move was to have our lawyer, Ray Koskie, obtain a decision from the Ontario Labour Relations Board that Zanini's collective agreement was illegal and thus null and void. Zanini had taken shortcuts during his organizing drive and we wanted the OLRB to decertify his group. This launched a three-way fight between Local 183, the Council of Concrete Forming Unions, and Zanini.

I put all of the Council of Concrete Forming Unions organizers on the Local 183 payroll except Tony Michaels, who had been an original ringleader of the council. Then I told our other representatives to forget any and all other problems of Local 183 except for the most serious grievances and instructed them to help these new organizers recruit the concrete formers.

Our organizers blitzed jobs sites, trying to sign up workers, while I visited forming contractors to get them to drop their opposition to our campaign. My pitch to them was that they could improve the stability of the industry by dealing with one large, well-established union that would not favour one contractor over another. Fed up with the chaos caused by inter-union fighting, they were happy to go along.

We avoided applying for certification at the OLRB so as not to give competing unions the opportunity to intervene and jam up the legal process. We chose another perfectly legal path and retained a respectable, professional, chartered accountant to audit and certify that we represented the majority of the bargaining unit employees by comparing our membership list to the contractor employees list. As soon as we reached a majority of workers in each company, we asked those companies to sign our collective agreement. Not one of our agreements was challenged by the other unions. By fall, all residential concrete forming contractors had been organized by Local 183. We added 1,000 members representing not just labourers but carpenters, rod men, cement finishers, and lay-out men.

Now, I have to say, we learned as we went along. During our concrete forming campaign, we applied to certify a company called Meridian. A few days later I got a phone call from Bruce Benning, a labour lawyer acting for the company.

"John, what do you have against our company?" he asked.

"Nothing," I replied, noting that we were out to organize all concrete forming contractors.

"But we are not a concrete forming contractor," replied Benning, "we are a high-rise builder!" High-rise builders sublet concrete forming structures to concrete forming contractors (the only exception was Del Zotto, now Tridel).

I must confess that my knowledge of the high-rise residential industry was then poor, to say the least. Benning arranged a meeting with the owner of Meridian, Max Merkur, at his office on the top floor of an apartment building he owned on Erskine Avenue. Max was a canny real estate investor. He had bought up huge areas of land to build apartments and still more land in North York off Bayview Avenue to build houses. In his office he proudly displayed a painting from the Group of Seven. It turned out that collecting art was his other passion. He was also married to a woman named Rita, an artist who painted in the abstract expressionist style of Jackson Pollock. Max had a reputation for being a hard and tough man to deal with. With me, however, he was friendly. He said he had nothing against unions but he did not want to be the only high-rise builder to be organized. I knew I had to quickly expand my knowledge of the high-rise building industry so I went to work. At that time there were five major developers doing the majority of residential high-rise construction. In addition to Meridian, there was Cadillac Development (later Cadillac-Fairview) Greenwin, Belmont, and Del Zotto.

Del Zotto was not only a builder but at that time also a forming contractor. Over the years, I met many times with one of the brothers and company directors, Elvio Del Zotto, a lawyer with his own law practice. He was liberal-minded and would later be the president of the Ontario wing of the Liberal Party of Canada.

Not only did he not oppose our organizing drive but within legal limits he tried to help.

Another surprise came a month after my meeting with Max Merkur. Harold Green, one of the principals with Greenwin Development invited me to a breakfast meeting at a restaurant on Wilson Avenue and Bathurst, which he claimed had the best bagels in the world. At first, I was reluctant to go. Harold was another man with a reputation for being difficult. I had met him only once, in 1969, during an event with the high-rise builders and the Toronto Building and Construction Trades Council. Anyway, the bagels sounded good so I decided to show up and after the initial ritual niceties about the weather and kids, Harold asked me point-blank: "Who is calling the shots at Local 183?"

"Harold," I replied, "you know I am the manager."

"We know that, but that's not what I asked."

It was a commonly held belief that while I was the manager in name, Gallagher was the power behind the throne. Some even thought it was Reilly. This distorted perception helped me for a number of years because being underestimated can be a blessing.

Harold was primarily concerned about Gallagher's past history of shutting down job sites. I quickly put Harold's fears to rest and he accepted that I was truly "calling the shots" at Local 183. A couple of weeks later, Harold invited me to lunch at a restaurant on Mount Pleasant Avenue just south of Eglinton. There I met representatives of the other high-rise builders: Ken Brokenhurst from Cadillac; Harold and Bill Proudfoot of Greenwin; Bev Howard from Meridian (later Erskine Construction); and Herb Stricken. The lunch was cordial but I was peppered with questions. I tried to answer all of them frankly and openly and at the end of the lunch, Harold, speaking on behalf of the group, said: "John, we are not against unions, but we want to deal with a union we can trust, a union that does not play games, and one with which we can have a constructive and productive relationship. It is up to our employees to decide, but we will inform our project managers and foremen not to oppose your organizing drive."

So I directed our organizers and representatives to organize not only concrete forming workers but also apartment builders' labourers. Within months, we signed our first collective agreement with the high-rise builders, covering a few hundred labourers, most of them employed to clean up construction materials and to perform the so-called final cleaning before people moved into the units. In time, this would prove to be Local 183's most important agreement. With Harold's assistance, we had been able to include a seniority clause for the builders' employees, which was unheard of in the construction industry. Harold was tough but he was not the heartless person some people may have thought he was. I got to know him as a very enlightened and humanitarian employer who over the years became a true friend and supporter of our union.

Some concrete forming contractors were more troublesome. They played games to sabotage our organizing drive. However, I was one step ahead of them thanks to great intelligence details passed on to me from a number of sources. One of them was the owner of a large lumberyard that supplied materials to the forming contractors. Let us just say that he was a friend of a good friend of mine and he did not really know that I was the end user of this intelligence. For example, I received some intel that a major concrete forming contractor who was playing games with our union was actually being controlled by a high-profile insurance company which had invested in his company. In fact, the company had invested so much and he was so indebted to it that it was calling the shots in his business to protect its money.

With my intelligence report, I went to the CEO of the insurance company and laid the cards on the table. It was in both our interests, I said, to co-operate. The industry was in chaos, contractors were undercutting each other, and no one was making any money, least of all their guy. If he signed with us, he would help us to create a level playing field. Everyone could compete fairly, there would be more opportunity to make money, and the insurance company's investment would be better protected. I struck a chord. Money guys understand one thing: money. They had no appetite for a construction industry fight. They just wanted to invest and mitigate risk.

This kind of intelligence was important because we were in a race against time, rushing to sign up the remaining concrete forming contractors before competing unions could do it. In September of that year, our International held its convention in Miami. I did not attend, although I was an elected delegate because our local's drive was so critical. I also recalled three of our delegates to Toronto to speed up our organizing.

In October 1971, Zanini admitted defeat and called the last membership meeting of his independent union at the Lansdowne Theatre. He announced that he was closing shop. Someone from the floor asked him what they should do and he replied: "Don't ask me, ask that man." He pointed toward our organizer, Chester De Toni, sitting in the audience. He had been sent by me to observe and report back. De Toni was invited up on the stage and naturally he invited everybody to join Local 183. I called De Toni our General MacArthur because he accepted the defeat of the enemy.

Earlier in my story, I noted that after I was fired by Zanini in 1960, Charlie Irvine prophesied: "Bruno, one day you will regret it!" And there you are. Call it what you want but karma has a way of balancing the book of life. I nevertheless want to acknowledge that whatever our differences, Irvine and Zanini played an important part in impressing upon Canada's early wave of Italian construction-working immigrants the need for unions and the necessity to fight for better conditions.

CHAPTER 15

THE RIGHT STUFF

Hamilton-based S. McNally and Sons was a major tunnel company operating in Toronto in the sewer and water-main sector. In 1970 it was awarded by the TTC a subway tunnel known as Y3 on Yonge Street just south of Highway 401. Its bid was substantially below others'. Previously, all subway tunnels had been done by the multinational Robert McAlpine, an English company which employed mostly Irish workers, so much so that back in England the Irish workers were called the McAlpine fusiliers.

A year later, Local 183 was renewing all of its civil engineering agreements but one company engaged in subway construction refused to sign: S. McNally of Hamilton. The firm objected to the bonuses received by the miners, whose incentives were like those of the miners working in the McAlpine tunnels. S. McNally wanted to eliminate the bonus while expecting the same productivity. The company added some other conditions that were totally unacceptable to us. The company shut down the project. We declared a strike. We were both within our rights. It was a classic standoff.

The major issue for us was that we could not allow one company to sign a different agreement from that which we had

negotiated with the Heavy Construction Association representing subway contractors of both the open-cut and tunnel variety.
One of our fundamental principles was to treat every contractor
the same. The standoff continued for months until one morning, November 29, 1971, I was reading the *Toronto Daily Star* at
home over a cup of coffee and came across a story about the
dispute. It was fairly balanced but problematic. Former Toronto
Mayor Ralph Day (1938–1940), who was then the TTC chairman
(1963–1972), accused our union of being responsible for the delay
and he made additional false claims against us.

We responded by picketing the TTC offices. We forced a
meeting with Day and explained our displeasure. The press gave
ample coverage to this escalation of the political dimensions of
the dispute and the provincial Ministry of Labour called for a
mediation meeting. In advance, I instructed our bargaining committee, composed of Irish miners, to lay off their usual wisecracks
and funny remarks during the session and to show the utmost
seriousness and restraint.

At the mediation, the labour relations representative engaged
by Pat and Joe McNally of S. McNally made a number of proposals that under normal circumstances would have resulted in us
walking away from the table. We kept our cool and embarked on
a strategy of our own. I asked many clarifying questions without
agreeing to or opposing the McNally proposals and without being
argumentative. I knew he was trying to push us into a corner
and blame us for not negotiating in good faith, so I just played
along.

At one point he said: "We want guaranteed production of six
feet per day!"

"Are you really sure?" I asked politely.

"You heard us!" Pat McNally exclaimed. "We are serious in
this negotiation."

"We are too," I replied. "If we weren't, we would have agreed
to your proposal because I am sure you meant six feet per shift

[which meant eighteen feet per day] not per day. We are trying to help you here."

That embarrassed and flustered Pat and Joe McNally, and started an argument between them. I took advantage of the momentary confusion to tell the government mediation officer, Gary Speranzini, that since the company could not make up its mind, we were leaving. The government officer looked lost as the McNallys continued squabbling. Down in the coffee shop, one of the lead miners, Chris McDonnell complimented me: "Your performance was better than Peter O'Toole!"

The TTC asked Doug Hamilton, a former Ontario Federation of Labour secretary treasurer and TTC commissioner, to intervene and settle the dispute. I knew Hamilton well and was comfortable with the choice. One day in early January 1972 he invited me to join him in a suite at the King Edward Hotel. I arrived early and there was Joe McNally. Joe almost immediately said he did not personally support the company proposals presented to us. He added that he was willing to sign the new collective agreement with one concession: the third shift on Saturday at midnight would stay at time and one half, rather than double as per the new agreement. I agreed. The whole thing lasted half an hour. Doug Hamilton thanked both of us and we left.

Much to my surprise, the miners almost rejected the compromise. I had a tough time explaining to them the whole city was looking at us and we could not afford to show inflexibility to the community. Finally, they understood and unanimously accepted it and the project was finished ahead of schedule. Sometimes, getting an agreement is as much about the people in the negotiations as it is about the members and the companies involved.

This played on my mind while traveling back and forth to the United States. I noticed the American locals were not as aggressive in organizing as we were, and most of them had few well-paid, full-time representatives. It struck me that the higher the salary, the fewer full-time representatives and organizers a local required.

To organize, a union requires the right bodies, not a lot of bodies. When I became the business manager I kept salaries, including mine, at a moderate level so that we could hire more representatives who could help to organize more members.

I was also frugal with our budget. When we had a good cash flow, we could have hired more people, expanded services, instituted new programs or built new headquarters. But what would happen when the cash flow got tight? I preferred to put our money into more organizing, telling our representatives: "Go out, police the jobs, and organize because if you don't there someday may not be enough money to pay your salaries." We also paid lower salaries (including mine) than other locals, although our membership was larger. It did not make me especially popular with the staff but it worked. Local 183 would not be what it is today if we had been content to sit on our behinds and just look after ourselves. Our philosophy was simple: "Take care of the members and the members will take care of you."

Hiring the right representative was always a big issue for me. I would keep certain criteria in mind with each hire. I would look at the nature of the sector we were working in, the work experience of a candidate in that sector, the ethnic composition of the membership, the candidate's union experience, attendance at union meetings, and, perhaps most important, his ability to stand up on his two feet and make decisions. I did not want a "yes man." I needed people who could think independently. Over the years, I must have hired more than fifty union representatives and I always took this approach.

For example, in 1970 my duties and responsibilities were many and diversified and at the time Jack Dillon was our representative servicing the tunnels, including the subway. Jack was an old Irishman, rough, of limited education, but with a lot of common sense and a good heart. He had worked as a miner before becoming a representative. He had one fatal weakness: he could not make a decision. Every time there was a problem, he would call me, explain the problem, discuss it with me, and ask for direction. Time was a luxury I did not have.

When we needed another representative as the subway side of things grew, I found the perfect candidate. Tom Connolly was a young lead miner and a couple of years earlier he had impressed me during a labour safety dispute with Robert McAlpine in subway construction. On that occasion, Gallagher had shut down the job over safety issues. McAlpine's labour relations man, Bill Gibson, had met with Gallagher and acceded to more than half of our requests but it was not good enough for Gallagher who wanted total victory. He pushed the members to continue the strike. Before the adjournment of the meeting, a member stood up and said: "Just a moment, Gerry, with all due respect to you, the company concessions are good enough for me. I propose we take a vote and go back to work." Gerry was hesitant and replied that it would take time to prepare the secret ballots. Tom then stood up and said: "We're all Irishmen here and we are not afraid to stand up and be counted!" Tom carried the day and the strike was over.

This is the man I need, I said to myself. So Tom was appointed. On his first day on the job, he called from the subway site with a problem and asked for direction. I knew that if I helped him through it, it would become his habit to call me and I was not going down that road again.

"Play it by ear, Tom," I said. There were a few moments of silence on the other end.

"I got it," replied Tom

He resolved the issue. In later years, he became an assistant manager both at Local 183 and at the Labourers International Union of North America Provincial Council. He was a great example to me of why you need to hire the right body, not just anybody.

CHAPTER 16

THE INVISIBLE PAYCHEQUE

In the modern world, the cash you receive from your paycheque is generally just a percentage of what you are earning in terms of value. Much of the hidden paycheque comes to you in the form of benefits. It was not always this way. Over many years, unions led the long and difficult fights to bring health and dental benefits to working men and women, and to ensure they have adequate pensions to carry them in their retirement. I am proud to have played my part in winning not just basic benefits but in bringing innovative and forward-thinking benefits for our members.

In 1971, Local 183 was successful in negotiating a five-cents-per-hour contribution to a newly established benefits plan, jointly administered with employers. Initially, the benefits were modest. They provided a small amount for life insurance and prescription drugs. In subsequent negotiations, we were able to increase the contributions and as we did the benefits were increased and expanded to cover doctors and hospital care, vision care, dental, sick pay, and more.

The road was not always easy. Sometimes our best intentions were undermined by our own people. Some members abused their sick pay benefits. During periods of unemployment, they were collecting both sick pay and Unemployment Insurance (now Employment Insurance) benefits from the federal government, sometimes getting more in total than they would have received if they were working. All they needed to do was get a doctor's certificate which was not that difficult in those days. Our benefits plan was jeopardized by this practice and we were going to have to either cut overall benefits or increase member contributions, which would have effectively reduced the hourly wages of our workers.

I went to the members and put forward this plan: we would report the name of any member collecting sick pay to the Unemployment Insurance office. "It is not fair," I told members at a meeting. "The majority pays for the abuses of a minority." The members approved it and this drastic action brought the benefits plan back to a healthy state.

When the Ontario government changed the Ontario Hospital Insurance Plan from a monthly fee to a wholly taxpayer supported system, we used the extra money to expand our benefits even more. In the 1980s, I introduced a bereavement benefit. The ability to take paid time from work following the death of a loved one is common in many sectors but not in the construction industry. We were the first construction union to include this benefit in our plan. It provided three days off with pay for dealing with the loss of an immediate family member. In time our benefits plan became one of the best in North America.

We were always looking for ways to improve it. In 1977, while attending a seminar of the International Foundation of Employees Benefit Plans, I learned that the New York firefighters' union, the Uniformed Fire Fighters Association, had its own dental clinic. "Why not us?" I asked. We had purchased the building next to our office on Dupont Street to renovate as a training centre. We now reserved space for a dental clinic, which was to be paid for and controlled by the benefit fund.

I consulted a dentist, Dr. Jim Lees, and our lawyer, Ray Koskie. The first issue was that we needed the approval of the Royal College of Dentistry. Accordingly, we prepared a plan and our lawyer approached the college for its blessing. It came back a clear no. The plan violated a college rule which said a dentist can only be employed by another dentist. This is perhaps the only profession in Ontario with a restriction of this nature.

At the outset, I was not going to take no for an answer. To me, it was about providing free dental care to our members and their families, most of them immigrants with many more children than the average family, and the Ontario Hospital Plan did not cover dentist's visits, which could get quite expensive. I turned to the Ontario Minister of Health, Dennis Timbrell, who was sympathetic to our cause. He told us that his father had been a member of our sister Local 506 while working in a brick factory. He went so far as to say that if the impasse was not resolved, he would introduce special legislation to allow the opening of our clinic. What is especially interesting is that this was under the Progressive Conservative government of Premier Bill Davis.

Timbrell undertook to speak to the dentists' college. Meanwhile, Koskie, in his legal research, pushed the opinion that the college rule was in violation of the Combines Investigation Act (now the Competition Act), a piece of federal legislation which regulated anti-competitive business practices. He said his own profession's regulatory body, the Law Society of Upper Canada, also had a similar rule on its books but that it had been abolished because it gave lawyers a monopoly and left them open to legal challenge.

With this political backing and legal opinion in hand, we met again with the Royal College of Dentistry. It knew in advance that we were prepared to take this matter all the way to the Supreme Court of Canada and it had a tough choice to make. This time, its representatives were more accommodating. They dropped their threat to suspend dentists practising at our clinic and together we found a way to operate, but they still refused to give us their official blessing. Instead, they simply turned a blind eye to our clinic.

By 1979, we were finally ready to open with the latest equipment and with good dentists and other qualified personnel standing by. The dentists were not on salaries but were paid a fee for work performed, based on a percentage of the Royal College fee schedule. All other expenses were paid by our fund. There were never any problems recruiting good dentists. Local 183 still has the only union dental clinic of this kind in Canada. The Canadian Auto Workers (now UNIFOR) established a dental clinic in Oshawa, but its structure is much different from ours, operating more as a co-op.

After health and dental benefits, the next big item for the long-term health and wellness of our members was a pension plan. In 1972, we negotiated a small contribution to be remitted by employers to the newly established Central and Eastern Canada Labourers Pension Fund. It had been set up by our International Labourers Union, and it was managed by union trustees appointed by the International. Toward the end of the 1970s, I was appointed as a trustee. Over time, pension contributions were substantially increased and so were the pension benefits to retiring members.

As a trustee, I was fascinated by the regular presentations of the money managers hired by the fund. Each had a different view of the economy and of how to invest our money. They helped me to better understand the intricate world of finance. After all, we were dealing with hundreds of millions of dollars and our decisions had a major impact on the members' benefits so it was important to be knowledgeable on investment issues.

The first chairman was the International's general secretary and treasurer Terrence O'Sullivan. He was succeeded by Arthur E. Coia, a former senior regional manager from New England.

Arthur was from the old school. He had a disarming smile but a mind like a steel trap. He was a labour leader who truly loved his union, having started in construction at the age of twenty and then been elected to New Providence Rhode Island Local 271 two years later in 1936. He was renowned for promoting education and training for construction workers and when he retired in 1989, the 500,000 members of LIUNA honoured him by establishing a scholarship fund in his name.

He came to Toronto often where his only mistake—a common one among Americans—was to consider Canada as just another state. He meant well but he did not understand that this was an affront to Canadian sensibilities. Can you imagine if a Canadian businessman went to the U.S. and acted as though Canada was in charge of everything?

Despite his confusion around geography and history, the two of us became good friends and he provided me with counsel and support.

* * *

It was as a trustee of the pension plan that I got myself into a pickle and it resulted in something I truly regret. After building our house in 1979, I could not manage our big mortgage. Rita, my wife, went back to work. She got a job at the pension fund. As an employee, she was represented by the Office Employee International Union. In the middle of the 1980s, during their contract negotiations, Arthur called and asked me to take over the negotiations of behalf of the plan. I refused on the grounds that it would present me with a conflict of interest. I would be negotiating against my wife. I recommended he leave negotiations in the hands of a trustee who was an International representative.

"If we leave it to him, we will have a strike for sure!" Arthur said. "We don't want that. You are the only one that can reach a reasonable settlement on our behalf!"

Reluctantly, I accepted. It was our family practice not to talk about business at home. We wanted an oasis of tranquillity behind our doors and one of the ways to achieve it was to keep business out. On a Saturday night, during a wedding reception, I summoned enough courage to ask my wife: "What do you people really want?"

"To be covered by the pension plan," she replied. I saw her point, and I was in agreement with what she wanted, but being obsessed with the conflict of interest, I conceded only minimal pension coverage during negotiations. A couple of years after, when our mortgage became more manageable, Rita quit her job. Unfortunately, when she reached retirement age, her pension benefits were minimal. The fact that I had used my considerable experience and knowledge in negotiations to agree to a minimal pension so as not to be perceived as doing something from which my wife could benefit made me feel terrible. I still regret it to this very day.

Still, the fund has done well for thousands of members and their families, my wife's situation notwithstanding. It gives me great satisfaction to know our members can retire with dignity and economic security.

Of course, benefits and pensions are critical to everyone, not only in construction, but in our sector we faced additional risks because the work is physical and dangerous and there is always the threat of being injured on the job. As such, we reached another important milestone in 1976 by securing a clause for the reinstatement of injured workers.

At that time, when a member was injured and went on leave under the terms of the Workmen's Compensation Board, he was replaced by a newly hired employee. Most employers were reluctant to rehire the injured worker when he was able to return because it meant getting rid of the new and presumably able employee. I began pushing employers to grant the right of injured workers to return to their jobs on recovery. At first, the employers thought I was using this item as a bargaining chip in negotiations to obtain some other concession. We were close to a strike deadline when Frank Giles, president of the Operating Engineers Local 793, who had already settled with the employers in question, came to see me. Frank, well respected by us and the employers, had a reputation as a straight shooter. We had coffee at a greasy spoon on Dupont Street just west of Perth Avenue.

"You are not serious about that clause," he told me bluntly. "What do you really want?"

"Frank," I replied, "we are deadly serious about injured workers. We want justice for them and we are ready to strike for it."

Frank knew I meant every word. We had known each other well for some time. I had a feeling that he had been sent on a fishing expedition by some key contractors. At the next negotiating meeting, we got what we wanted. We were the first construction union to negotiate the reinstatement of injured workers and this clause was then included in many other collective agreements in the construction industry.

You see, it is not just about the money. There are so many other things that are important and vital to a working person's health and well-being. This is why the language in collective agreements is just as important as monetary issues, and sometimes more important.

The subcontractor clause is another example. This clause requires the main contractor to sublet work only to other union contractors. When we included this clause with builders of both the low-rise and high-rise variety, it became a real strength of the local for residential construction. As a rule, builders do not do the work themselves, they sublet everything. The clause ensures that concrete forming, concrete and drain, house basement, house framing, and bricklaying were to be all subcontracted to employers who had agreements with our local. This not only blocked non-union contractors but also those competing contractors who had formed alliances with other unions.

The cross-over clause was yet another item I came up with and negotiated into all of Local 183's collective agreements. Each union agreement specifies the type of construction to which it is applicable. The sewer and water-main agreement, for instance, is limited to sewer and water-main construction. What if a sewer and water-main company wants to build a bridge? Technically it could use non-union workers. Or it could use the hourly rates and conditions in the sewer and water-main agreement which are inferior to those in the heavy construction agreement. The cross-over clause states that if an employer is engaged in work other than the work specified in the collective agreement, but within the jurisdiction of the union local, the employer is bound by the terms and the conditions of the collective agreement applicable for that type of work.

A related and similarly important clause was the composite crew clause in the concrete forming agreement. The clause prevented forming contractors from subletting part of the work performed by the composite crew to other subcontractors, thus preserving the composite-crew concept which makes the residential forming industry in Toronto unique, productive, and more economical than this type of construction is in other North American jurisdictions.

These are just some examples of the language I negotiated in collective agreements. If you skipped some of the details here, I do not blame you. It is not the sexiest of subjects and not everyone is as passionate about it as I am but these non-cash benefits and assurances are of vital importance to workers and few workers go through their lives without at one time or another being thankful for their existence.

CHAPTER 17

AT WAR WITH WASHINGTON

The campaign to organize the concrete forming industry in 1971 drained the bank account of Local 183. With winter approaching, remittances of union dues from employers were substantially reduced so we did what every business has to do in lean times: we cut costs, paring everything down to what was most essential. Even with that, we were barely getting by. At the end of the year we were forced to postpone sending our monthly per capita transfer to the International, headquartered in Washington. It was a considerable sum and not sending it was a serious breach of the union's constitution.

The breach came at a difficult time. The International wanted to establish a pension plan for Ontario and Eastern Canada. It was intended to be completely under U.S. control with contributions coming from employers as part of the contract agreement with locals like ours. My objection was simple: the money was coming from our members and we wanted to control the pension plan here in Canada. Reilly was then manager of the Ontario Labourers District Council and he reported my objection to the

International in an unflattering light. Washington went ahead and announced the plan with the Hamilton Local. The entire general executive board of the international was set to travel to Hamilton to underscore the importance of the occasion.

It was a difficult time for me personally, as well. In the spring of 1972, Rita was pregnant with our second child. While we were visiting my relatives in North Bay during the Easter season, our car was rear-ended by another vehicle. We were worried for the health of the baby. To make matters worse, Rita had to undergo breast surgery. The doctor decided it was in her best interest to go ahead with the procedure despite a risk to her pregnancy. We knew consequences could be serious and we were under considerable stress.

In the midst of all this drama, I had received a phone call from Peter Fosco, president of our International from 1968 through 1975 (later, after his death, he was succeeded for two decades by his son, Angelo). His secretary had tracked me down at the hospital and put me on hold after curtly telling me, "The general president wants to speak to you."

I was at Rita's bedside and I was annoyed at the intrusion. Can you imagine anyone, today, boss or co-workers, calling anyone while they are in the middle of a family matter like a birth or surgery or even a funeral, and demanding to talk business? I was stretched to the limit between work and personal family matters and I was furious. The pressures of work meant I was stealing time from my family. Back then this was standard operating procedure but that did not mean I did not resent it.

Fosco was an old man and he was quite pleasant on the phone which calmed me down a bit. "Look," he said. "We will be in Hamilton on Sunday with the general executive board and we'd like to meet with you and your executive board. Our Canadian vice-president will call you about it, but don't tell him I called you first. I'm sure we can work out our differences."

Just as he said, the Canadian vice-president called me the following day. He was a man for whom I had little time. I thought he was incompetent. He had barely finished telling me about the Hamilton meeting when I snapped "I know" and hung up. I was still upset about Rita, so perhaps I was a little short.

I called a special executive board meeting of Local 183 and brought everyone up to speed. We decided to play along and participate in the International's pension plan but to ask Washington to waive our per capita dues for three months. That Sunday at precisely 10 a.m., I accompanied Mike O'Brien, the secretary treasurer of Local 183, and Frank Palazzolo, an executive board member, to the banquet hall where the launch of the Internationals' pension fund was to be celebrated. The place was closed.

Not knowing what else to do, we hung around, thinking we might be early. About an hour later, Henry Mancinelli, the business manager of the Hamilton local, showed up and asked us why we were not meeting with Fosco.

"That's why we're here!" I said.

"Not here," he said. "They're waiting for you at the Royal Connaught Hotel in Hamilton."

We had wrongly assumed that the meeting was going to take place at the hall. We had to scramble to find the address of the Connaught and to get there. Although we arrived just fifteen minutes after talking with Mancinelli, we were an hour and fifteen minutes late. Fosco was furious and in no mood to listen to our excuses.

"Shut up!" he screamed at me. "We've had enough of your games. We will put the local under trusteeship and get rid of you!"

Well, we were shocked. A deep silence gripped the room. In addition to ourselves, Gerry Gallagher and Jack Dillon were there, having driven down together. Gallagher knew Hamilton well, having first arrived from England to settle in Burlington. He had found the meeting without any trouble.

It was a humiliating experience. When we finally left the Connaught to go to the banquet hall, we found that nobody dared to speak to us or be around us. We were the skunk at the garden party. I was furious. I resented Fosco's threat after I'd given my life to the union and made untold sacrifices to defeat the formation of an independent Canadian union, which would have spelled the end for International building unions operating in Canada. I was also insulted on behalf of our membership.

On our return to Toronto, O'Brien and I held a meeting to decide our next move. First thing Monday morning we went to the bank and secured a loan to pay the arrears of the per capita tax in an effort to neutralize an issue that could put Local 183 in trusteeship. We sent the money super-express delivery to Washington that day but on Wednesday we got a registered letter from Terry O'Sullivan, secretary treasurer of the International, advising us that we were in a serious violation of the union constitution over the unpaid per capita tax and that they would be taking drastic action against us. I immediately sent a telegram telling him there was a lack of communication with his office because we had already paid the per capita tax. A few years after all this, I was told that it was the International's intention not to cash our cheque so as to bolster its case against us and allow it to take us over. Someone in their office screwed up, or, more likely, just did his job and cashed the cheque and we dodged a bullet.

The International was not done with us, however. A couple of days after, we were notified that its controller and his assistant were going to carry out an audit of our books and it was our duty to give them "our full cooperation." Sure enough, the following week the controller and his assistant arrived and spent a week at our office checking the books. After they left, they were required to attend a special meeting in Washington to discuss their findings and our situation.

A few days before this meeting, O'Brien suggested I call Fosco and try to explain again why we had been late for the meeting and offer an apology. "The old man looked genuinely hurt by our perceived lack of respect," he said. I was hesitant at first but I followed O'Brien's suggestion. I played phone tag with Fosco for a couple of rounds but then I found myself on the phone with him and he was charming. I told him what had happened and said I was sorry. He was all smiles and benevolence, telling me we must work together and, of course, I wholeheartedly agreed. It was an enormous relief. The general president, empowered by the union constitution, wields a big stick and a good working relationship with him is essential to providing the local union membership with the best representation.

I was later told by a source in Washington that the controller had found everything in order, leaving the International no avenue to pursue further action against us. And, in the 1980s, long after Fosco had passed, and with his son in charge, I ran into the controller at a conference in San Diego. He told me he had been surprised how good our records were. In the U.S., he said, his audits of local unions almost always resulted in trusteeship. He recalled meeting with the Canadian representative of the International at the King Edward Hotel after he had been through his books. The man had been disappointed to learn everything was in order. He even asked the controller to "create" something to justify trusteeship. The controller, a man of professional integrity, refused.

Before the year of our audit was over, I was asked to meet over a drink with Terry O'Sullivan, the secretary treasurer of the International. I was a little apprehensive. Terry was a former Marine, tall and well built. He was in Toronto as chairman of the newly established pension plan and we met at the King Edward. I asked Gallagher to join us, thinking their shared Irish heritage would melt some ice.

Terry came out swinging, immediately reading the riot act to me and emphasizing the power of the International as a warning not to mess with its authority. I stood firm and reminded him there was a border between Canada and the U.S. We would co-operate, I said, but we would not be dictated to. Gallagher told me afterwards things started off so heatedly that he was bracing for a fistfight. Terry was tough but fair and he changed his tone as we went over the issues. By the end of the night, we had become friends.

O'Sullivan and I forged a constructive relationship which, unfortunately, lasted only a short period. He had resigned by 1975. The International held a lunch in his honour in Chicago which I attended. After his farewell speech, he came down from the stage. There was a space around him and I walked towards him to wish him good luck: "Terry, now that we understand each other you are leaving!" He smiled and shook my hand. In 1999, his son Terence M. O'Sullivan became president of the International, a position he holds today.

On a happier note, our second child, Lisa, was born on June 3, 1972. Everything turned out well. Afterwards the doctor came out to congratulate me because at that time fathers were generally not welcome in the delivery room. The first thing I asked was, "How is the baby?"

"Fine."

"And the mother?"

"Fine also."

"Thank you, Doctor."

He looked at me and said: "What kind of a father are you?"

"Why?"

"Don't you want to know if it's a girl or a boy?"

"Oh yes, Doctor, what is it?"

I was so relieved that everything had gone well and that our fears over the car accident and surgery were groundless that I had forgotten to ask the gender.

"It's a girl!" he said, and then walked away looking somewhat disgusted with me.

CHAPTER 18

FIRING A UNION STEWARD

In the spring of 1973, one of our job stewards, Mario Penariol, was fired. He was working on an open-cut subway project on Yonge Street and York Mills for a company called Kilmer Van Nostrand, one of the companies run by Larry Tanenbaum, a major player in Toronto construction and later a part-owner of Maple Leaf Sports and Entertainment, which in turn owns the Toronto Maple Leafs, the Toronto Raptors, the Toronto Argonauts Football Club, and Toronto FC.

Mario was not a fanatical union militant. He was a hard worker and a common-sense person who just wanted safety and union rights to be respected by management. He was also the victim of a conflict of personalities. The superintendent of the project, Italo, had a bit of a Napoleon complex. He resented any interference with his right to manage and one day it came to a showdown and Mario was fired. The members respected Mario and demanded his reinstatement. We, as a union, considered our job stewards to be sacred cows, and our collective agreements contained clauses to protect them. They were to be one of the last employees laid off at the completion of a project, for example, and short of assaulting a boss or being caught red-handed stealing building materials, the shop stewards were to be handled with respect and left alone. Of course, I immediately tried to correct this injustice.

I contacted Larry Tanenbaum, who had learned the ropes from his father, Max, another icon of the Toronto construction scene. I knew Larry well. Father and son both operated on a handshake basis. You have to respect a man whose word is his bond. In this case, however, Larry said it was nothing personal, no hard feelings, but he had no choice. He had to back his supervisor who was doing a good job. My only legal option was to file a grievance and take the matter to private arbitration, as stipulated by the collective agreement. The problem was that it was a lengthy procedure and not fully understood by our members who wanted an immediate resolution.

Instead, I closed down the project, hoping Larry would take the hint and use the opportunity to reach a reasonable compromise. This strategy had worked in the past when Gallagher was running things and I had used the same option, when warranted. Times, however, were changing. Many companies were stiffening their resolve and using the law to fight back. Shutting down a project was a violation of the no-strike or lock-out clause in the collective agreement. It constituted an illegal strike.

Tanenbaum's company chose to fight and applied to the Ontario Labour Relations Board for a cease-and-desist order which, of course, it won. After a couple of days, I had no choice but to tell the members to return to work without Mario's reinstatement. We gambled and lost and it left a bitter taste in their mouths because they did not really understand the legal aspects.

Still, justice sometimes only takes time. About a year later, we certified the construction workers at a new condo project called Palace Pier on Lake Ontario. The developer was Larry Tanenbaum and this time we played it smart. We went to the company and tabled our proposals for a collective agreement, one I was pretty sure they would reject, and reject it they did. As a result, they gave us the right to legally strike after going through the lengthy process of conciliation. We put up pickets on the job site and closed it down.

The company's next move was to apply to join the Metropolitan Toronto Apartment Builders Association. As a member, it would be considered bound by the existing collective agreement between the association and Local 183. We would have had no choice but to return to work. Fortunately, I had one more trick up my sleeve. It was a rarely used legal procedure which stipulated that for the company to be covered by the collective agreement with the association, the other party, our union, had to agree in writing.

Usually, our agreement was just a formality but I wrote to the Metropolitan Toronto Apartment Builders Association that in this instance we would not agree to be bound by the collective agreement with this particular company and that we planned to keep its project closed down.

A couple of days later, I got a call from Harold Green of Greenwin, who was acting as the association spokesman. We had our usual bagel breakfast at the usual restaurant on Wilson and Bathurst. "Look," Harold said, "you cannot do this to our association. We have certain principles and reputations to uphold." Harold was morally right but I gave him the background of Mario's firing which was at the root of our dispute with Larry.

"Okay," he said, "I'll give you a few days—two or three max— then you take down the picket line and agree to be bound by our agreement."

We shook hands. It was a gentlemen's agreement. Two days later, Stan Dinsdale, the labour lawyer for Kilmer Van Nostrand, called me to meet him at his Bay Street office. I walked into the library and found Larry Tanenbaum waiting for me.

"I'll leave the two of you alone," said Dinsdale as he made his exit. "This is a political matter not a legal one."

When we were alone, Larry looked at me and said, "I am ready to take your steward back."

He was a man of few words and this was typical of him, getting straight to the point.

"Fine," I replied. "With retroactive pay."

Larry looked at me for a few seconds and nodded: "Less any money he got from unemployment insurance."

"Agreed," I said, and we shook hands.

It was all done in a few minutes. In this kind of dispute, it all comes down to the integrity of the parties. Larry was a fair employer. He kept his hands out of the bargaining talks and always respected our union. We reciprocated that respect.

Reputation is everything for a union. That is one of the principals we held to in organizing our workers and it was one of the prime reasons why we became the largest construction local in Canada. We knew the rules of the game and we made the right choices at the right time.

For example, we applied in 1973 to certify a company pouring sidewalks for the city of Toronto. As soon as we filed the paperwork, all twenty employees were fired. The company tried to camouflage this action by saying it was closing down operations but its foreman made it quite clear that the crew was being punished for joining a union. At that time, before I helped change the law, the onus was on the union to prove that an employee had been fired for union activities, which required a lengthy legal process before the Ontario Labour Relations Board. I did not have that kind of time. Our reputation was at stake. I could not allow the sidewalk company to get away with firing these men without undermining everything we stood for as a union.

We took a good look at the contractor's operations and found that it was also working for a major sewer and water-main development company that was developing subdivisions. The developer was a non-union company we had dealt with back in the 1970 strike in the sewer and water-main sector. We had used our strikers, together with Local 793 of the Operating Engineers, to picket non-union companies, including this company, without success.

I remembered a twist to that story that I could use to our advantage. I recalled that one morning Gerry Gallagher had called me into his office and said that he had received a visit from a person reputed to be a member of organized crime: "He brought me a case of whiskey and asked me to leave that [sewer and water-main] company alone. Here is the whiskey, give it to the boys on the picket lines." Now, fate had it that Frank Giles of the Operating Engineers had that very morning taken the pickets off the company in question because they had done nothing to stop the non-union employees from going to work. It was no big loss. Sometimes you have to fold and put your resources to better use. But it looked like we had taken the hint, and the whiskey, and pulled our pickets.

Fast-forward to 1973, and I have just finished reading the book *The Godfather*. I was inspired. Business is business, I thought. Let us have a conversation. I called the owner of the company, asking to meet. He invited me to his home at 8:30 p.m. that evening. I brought one of our representatives, Lou Castaldo, and when we arrived the contractor invited us into his library and offered us some good cigars and fine cognac.

"I thought you would come alone," he said.

I told him that I trusted Lou but if he preferred I would ask him to leave.

"No," he replied, "if you trust him it's okay with me. What can I do for you?"

"Well," I said, "over the last few years we left you alone but now we have a problem."

I went on to explain what the sidewalk company had done to our new members and told him how it would damage our reputation. I told him that the sidewalk company was now one of his subcontractors and I was looking for a way to balance things out.

I did not come out and say that I thought his company and my union had an understanding dating back to that case of whiskey. I knew what he was thinking, however.

He looked at me for a while and said, "Now that I think about it, they are doing substandard work for us. Tomorrow we will terminate their contract."

We shook hands and left. The sidewalk company declared bankruptcy. Our members went to work for another unionized sidewalk company which completed the city contract.

A few years later we successfully organized this particular developer's company. The owner always treated our members with respect and we never had another problem.

CHAPTER 19

A DIRTY BUSINESS

The years 1968 to 1972 were filled with tension and strife in the construction industry. With new technologies like drywall pushing some workers and companies out of business, and with intense competition between developers and unions, it was what one observer called "a propitious time for illegal activities." The Metropolitan Toronto Police logged four incidents of threats, 234 of wilful damage, fifteen of assault, twenty-three of arson, and five explosions as well as uncounted thefts and break-ins related to construction throughout that time. There were reports of apartment buildings being burned down and of screws being loosened on construction scaffolding, among other acts of sabotage. One union local hired a former professional boxer with no previous labour experience as a "business agent." The exterior of a Toronto lathing company was strafed with bullets from semi-automatic weapons, and later dynamited. "The construction business," one contractor later testified, "is not a lily-white business, as we all know."

In 1972, Dr. Morton Shulman, an NDP Member of Ontario's Provincial Parliament, began raising in the legislature allegations of criminal corruption involving contractors and a number of building trades unions, particularly in the drywall and tile and terrazzo industries. Later he expanded his horizons to the concrete forming industry. His constant hammering at these issues left the Ontario government of Conservative Premier Bill Davis no option but to call a Royal Commission to investigate the charges. It was known formally as the Royal Commission on Certain Sectors of the Building Industry, and informally as the Waisberg Commission, named after the judge who presided over it, Harry Waisberg. The commission was established in 1973 and it added more controversy and conflict to the industry because everyone was under the microscope.

One of the catalysts for Shulman's tirades was the shooting of Bruno Zanini. I remember one afternoon in the summer of 1972 I got a call from someone saying he was Bruno Zanini's son and demanding to know why I had shot his father. I thought it was a prank and hung up but the next day I read in the newspaper that Zanini had in fact been shot in the leg in the basement garage of an apartment building on the afternoon of August 23. At this point in his life, Zanini had been unsuccessfully involved in trying to organize workers in concrete forming and other sectors. He had been convicted of possession of burglary tools after driving two accomplices to a home where they broke in. However, he appealed his conviction all the way to the Supreme Court of Canada, where his lawyer argued that Zanini should never have been convicted of possession of burglary tools because there was never any finding that there were burglary tools in his possession. In October 1967 the Supreme Court of Canada in *Zanini v. The Queen, [1967] S.C.R. 715* agreed, setting aside the conviction and upholding the appeal. And now Zanini was back and very much involved in the trade union movement. I'll let the Waisberg Commission tell the story:

That very morning Zanini had been talking to Romeo Di Battista to raise money. Zanini described it as money to be advanced by Di Battista for union organization, while Di Battista described it as an ordinary loan sought by Zanini. As Zanini was the only eyewitness, it would be fair to use his own words to describe what took place.

> Mr. Zanini: 'I couldn't see very much, I could just see so much of the side of his face, looked smooth, I could see he was dark hair, sort of a little bit of a tinge of olive oil complexion but he was scruffy, maybe a long beard or big beard, something hasn't shaved, and that's as far as it went. I didn't pay any more attention.'
>
> Mr. Shepherd (Commission Counsel): 'And you didn't see the other man at all other than to realize there was a man there?'
>
> A: 'There was two of them, one was very dark complexion, the one that turned his back to me was fair. I imagine he was about 5 foot 9, the fellow in the dark complexion that came towards me, he was sort of a slight—maybe 5 foot 6 or seven.'
>
> Q: 'Would it be correct to say you told the police on their arrival that one man was as you have described, and really all you can say about the other man was that he was male and he was white; is that correct?'
>
> A: 'That's correct.'
>
> Q: 'What did you do?'
>
> A: 'I proceeded to my car, 287, the slot where I had my car, got into it and the car just wouldn't start. I did it four times, what the heck comes here. As I stepped out there was a fellow with a flashlight kept putting it in my face. I paid no attention, I thought maybe it was a joke or something, so I just don't pay any attention but just as I got in front of my door, he was twelve feet approximately, give and take, I couldn't say for sure, Mr. Shepherd, I figure around that and the flashlight was constantly in my face. He said, "Hold it. Don't Move." Ping, Ping. It was all over.'
>
> Q: 'You indicate two sounds?'
>
> A: 'Yes.'

Q: 'Are you hearing two shots or one shot and on echo?'

A: 'Well, you know, I am practically deaf in my right ear. I heard ping, ping, just like that.'

Q: 'Did you feel something strike you?'

A: 'Oh, yes, very sharp and my leg just buckled and I went down. Then all of a sudden, just seeing like that, and I turned around and looked and the fellow got into the station-wagon and they drove away. I looked, it was a white-coloured one with a purple or red stripe in the centre right across the body.'

Q: 'And that's all he said to you, just "Hold it"?'

A: '"Hold it, don't move." Ping, ping, that was the end.'

After the shooting someone phoned his apartment and told his sons that he had just been shot. The children arrived immediately armed for battle, but of course the assailants had fled. Zanini expressed his views as follows.

Mr. Shepherd: 'Can you assist us as to anything else surrounding the events of the shooting itself, or do I have it all now?'

Mr. Zanini: 'Well, leading to the shooting, why I was shot—or was this what you are referring to Mr. Shepherd? I have ideas why I was shot, but I am not certain. And I am not sure as to the reasons why they wanted to shoot me, the motives.'

Q: 'So long as it is understood it is your surmise, is it correct to say that your surmise is that someone in the labour movement resented your activities in going about speaking to the men?'

A: 'And the contractors.'

Q: 'And the contractors as well?'

A: 'Positive. Positive. That is why the contractors are all paying the men right now. There is no chiselling going on because this Royal Commission is sitting.'

Zanini claimed he was shot to keep him quiet about the corruption he was investigating in the concrete forming industry and

Dr. Shulman backed him up. The commission later heard wiretap evidence that a bouncer by the name of Frank "Angel" Veltri had been paid $1,500 for the shooting.

* * *

In reaction to all this, the Ontario government expanded the Royal Commission's terms of reference to include the concrete forming industry and Local 183. We found ourselves the first to be investigated and police officers came, took all kinds of records from our union office, and called many of our representatives to be questioned separately. I guess they were a little frustrated because they could not find anything wrong. They even apparently asked one of our representatives: "How do you hide money in the local?"

All kinds of people were saying all kinds of things but no one could prove anything. For example, in the spring of 1973 we held an election for the office of president, which is really an honorary position with a lot of respect accorded to the person who occupies it. Carl Filipazzo ran and lost against Gerry Gallagher and he turned around and complained to the Waisberg Commission about all kinds of skulduggery during the vote and the ballot counting. Filipazzo, being Italian and knowing the majority of members were also Italians, could not accept that they did not vote for him. What he really did not want to accept was that Gerry had a fine reputation and that, with my strong support, he had won the election fair and square.

We were forced to reconstruct for the police all the details of the election and the process we had followed. As it turned out they were duly satisfied with our supporting evidence and accepted that the election was truly free and fair. Many contractors and union representatives, including myself and others, were called to testify at the Waisberg Commission. Some approached their testimony with caution but I saw it as an opportunity to table some of my thoughts on trade unions and organizing construction workers.

Around that time, I had been sponsored by our International to attend a three-month trade union study program at Harvard University. The course was extremely interesting and I learned many things, including how U.S. labour laws came about and how other jurisdictions approached labour legislation and practices. Most impressive was the Australian model where labour strife is kept at a minimum with a system that sees most disputes settled by labour boards. I also learned that our union constitution required a local election every three years, a district council election every four years, and an international election every five years because the whole system was based on American labour law. At our next International convention, I submitted a resolution, which was adopted, that local elections be held every four years if permitted by law. It also led me to present to Judge Waisberg some research which had a dramatic impact on labour law in Ontario.

Upon my return to Toronto from Harvard, I was called by the commission counsel, a Mr. Sheppard. I went with our lawyer, Ray Koskie, and Sheppard congratulated us on our record keeping, noting that they found nothing wrong with our activities. He encouraged me to carry on along the same path.

There was a good reason why our books were in order. In 1968, when I was the secretary treasurer, I hired accountant Al Resnick to give us an opinion on our record keeping. He was blunt: our records were not only unacceptable, but they could be open to unpleasant interpretation. "Not only must you do the right things," he added, "but you must be in a position to prove yourself impeccably clean." Transparency was the rule. We hired him to straighten our system and tasked him to be vigilant and critical on anything and everything. He did what we asked and over the years we benefited from his work and our self-imposed discipline.

Unfortunately, a number of contractors in the drywall, tile and terrazzo businesses and some union representatives, including Bruno Zanini and Charlie Irvine, did not come out too well. They were taking payments from contractors, selling out the workers they represented. Here are some excerpts from the Waisberg Commission:

> There is evidence that the following union agents received payments from employers under circumstances that involved the interests of their employees who, at the time, were the principals of the union agents.

Mr. Justice Waisberg also took the time to detail his observations on some of the other characters:

> I found Agostino Simone to be an unusual character. On the one hand, he truly reflected the members of his union, Lathers Local 562. On the other hand, however, he did not seem disturbed by the fact that he had personally profited from his position. He admitted receiving a number of substantial payments from contractors who, at the time, had collective agreements with his union. In his evidence he told of a proposed interest in Romanelli's business; he described meetings of the lathing and dry wall contractors where money was collected for him. He told of contributions to the building of his home, and of freezers that were given to him and Frank Fior by a contractor.

Mr. Justice Waisberg continued:

> On 8 December 1969, Inspector Dorigo, who at that time was investigating the violence in the concrete forming sector of the building industry, interviewed Zanini. Simone had stated that Di Lorenzo had made a payment of $1500 to Zanini which had been delivered to him by Di Lorenzo's foreman, George Orla. After some

discussion, Zanini did admit to Dorigo that he had in fact received
such a payment. The evidence of Inspector Dorigo was presented
earlier in the discussion of the Leader office fire. It reveals that Di
Lorenzo paid money to Zanini.

A number of charges were laid as a result of the Waisberg
Commission investigation but not a single concrete forming
contractor with a collective agreement with our local was ever
accused of any wrongdoing nor were any of our union representatives. With a good relationship established with the judge and
the commission counsel, I thought I would offer them some of
the insight I had gained at Harvard. I had written my term paper
on the evolution of the concrete forming industry in Toronto and
its impact on the International Building Trades Unions. When
preparing the term paper, I asked Harold Green for his assistance
with the technical aspects of construction. He was very pleased
to oblige. I sent a copy of the paper to Judge Waisberg who was
quite intrigued and asked me if he could include it in his final
report.

At Harvard, I reflected on the Australian system and I asked
our lawyer, Ray Koskie, to prepare a brief for Judge Waisberg asking
for changes to Ontario labour law which would reflect its certification and grievance settlement systems. The most important
requests were: to reduce the percentage needed for an automatic
certification from 65 per cent to 55 per cent; to put the onus on
employers to prove employees were not fired for union activities
and not the other way around (this seems simple but in law it is a
very important difference and it is of great help to unions during
organizing campaigns); for construction grievances to be settled
as quickly as possible by the Ontario Labour Relations Board (at
that time, the Ontario Federation of Labour published a booklet
called *Justice Delayed Is Justice Denied* and we made it part of our
brief); and that the parent union organization must show just
cause for placing a local under trusteeship.

I still remember as if it were yesterday when Koskie and I met Judge Waisberg in his office to present our brief. The judge was a fair person who agreed with us on almost every point. He fully endorsed our proposal for the settlement of construction grievances saying he had acted as an arbitrator in Sudbury and was aware of how long private arbitration took and how expensive it was, making it impractical in the construction industry. The reality was, by the time the process is completed, so is the project and the company may well be out of business. He disagreed only with our last request. In his opinion, a local was the branch of a multinational corporation, which had the right to impose supervision.

Having filed my papers with Judge Waisberg, I did not expect that much would happen. How wrong I was. The Conservative Government of Ontario under Premier Bill Davis took Waisberg's recommendations seriously, enshrining most of them as amendments to the Ontario Labour Relations Act. The most important was the introduction of Section 124 (now Section 133), dealing with union grievances. In the past it took months if not years to take a grievance through private arbitration and was quite expensive. Section 124 stated that "notwithstanding" the language of a collective agreement, either party can take a grievance to the Ontario Labour Relations Board and have a hearing within fourteen days from the date of application and, at that time, at no cost. No other jurisdiction in North America has such progressive legislation to this day.

If the leaders of the Brandon Hall Group had had the foresight to propose such legislation at the earlier Goldenberg Commission they might still be around today. They chose instead to disregard the law. Their demise proves that over the long run it is far more beneficial to everyone for leaders to work with the law, and to work to change the law if they find it unsatisfactory. All construction and building unions in Ontario greatly benefited from this new legislation. The construction industry gained stability and improved labour relations from these changes. I am proud of the role I played to drive that change and some of the other changes that passed into the Ontario Labour Relations Act and to this day I consider it my significant contribution to the labour movement.

CHAPTER 20

LOCAL 183 IN ADOLESCENCE

Time did not stand still during the Waisberg Commission. Local 183 was busily expanding into both the high-rise and low-rise residential housing sectors. Our big break came when we succeeded in organizing companies like Cadillac Development that operated in both high-rise and low-rise projects. We expanded our collective agreement that governed their high-rise work to their low-rise townhouses, detached, and semi-detached dwellings. There was strong resistance from these big firms because they did not want to be the only house builders unionized. Most Ontario home builders were non-union at the time so we had to commit to organizing all GTA house builders to put everyone on a level playing field. It was not easy but over the years we succeeded in organizing most of the sector.

Having established a beachhead in low-rise housing, we noticed another sector that needed to be organized: house basement construction. In the 1960s, house basement construction changed from blocks to concrete forming with poured concrete. Low-rise concrete forming is different from high-rise, in terms of skill, materials, and method. In a house basement there is no steel reinforcing. It consists of assembling forms, usually four feet by eight feet, which are placed on footings to create the house walls. Then you pour concrete, letting it set. Afterwards, you dismantle the forms to use again. It is heavy, hard work, and more so back then because the forms were carried manually, often in adverse conditions such as rain or sleet, which would create mud that added to the weight.

The industry employed between eight hundred and a thousand workers, mostly Portuguese immigrants. When we started our campaign, we had a few successes but also some failures. The biggest company by far was Tru-Wall Concrete Forming, which was listed on the Toronto Stock Exchange. It alone employed more than three hundred workers. We signed up 45 per cent of Tru-Wall employees, enough for a vote, perhaps, but only if we considered the foremen to be management and excluded them from the bargaining unit. The company, of course, maintained that these were working foremen and, as such, they had to be included in the bargaining list. This was the first battle to be fought.

When a job category is in dispute, the OLRB appoints an officer to verify the function of the employee. Our strategy was to prolong the questioning of each employee in the process. There were more than forty foremen. The longer they were tied up in questioning, the more expensive it was in time for the company. Without their foremen on-site, crews were idle. I then called the company's owner, Leonard Ursini, a sharp businessman with a great sense of humour. "Lenny," I said, "if we carry on with these procedures, the only winners are the lawyers." Both of us had a lawyer present during the questioning of each foreman. "Why don't you give us voluntary recognition?" I asked. "You know we have signed a majority of your employees."

It was a bit of a bluff. The number of employees who have joined a union is kept secret by the OLRB. All the same, Lenny did not know how many we had signed. He looked at me and then wrote the names of all sixteen Toronto-area house basement contractors on a sheet of paper and said: "When you have organized these sixteen contractors, come back to me and I will give you voluntary recognition."

I accepted the challenge although, truthfully, I had no choice. And it was not as dire as it looked. We had already signed half of them. A few months later, I returned to Lenny and told him that I had been able to sign all but three companies on the list. He took a look, deleted two out of the three, and said: "These two are not that important but this one, Star Wall, is my major competition."

Without Lenny's company we could not establish a collective agreement for the house basement sector because he represented about half of the industry and other contractors would vigorously oppose unionization as putting them at a competitive disadvantage. So I personally dug into Star Wall and found out that one of its biggest clients was Academy Homes, at the time the fourth largest house builder in the region. It so happened that one of the owners of Academy Homes was my good friend and best man, Primo Di Luca. Naturally, I went over to see Primo to ask for his help. It did not start well.

"Are you crazy?" Primo yelled at me. "Every time you people organize an industry it costs us more to build."

I kept at him, however, and a few days later Primo organized a dinner at the Henry VIII restaurant in the old Skyline Hotel. Joining us was Luigi Aceto, the owner of Star Wall and one of his associates. It was cordial and we spoke about everything except union business. At the end of the evening, after taking care of the bill, Primo turned to Luigi and said: "Luigi, are you happy working for me?"

"You are the best builder we are working for!" stated Luigi.

"Do we pay you on time?" he asked.

"No complaints," Luigi replied.

"Well," Primo continued, "if you like to work for me, I am afraid that you also have to get along with my friend John."

Luigi understood immediately and asked me what he was supposed to do. "It's simple," I said. "Just make clear to your employees that you have nothing against our union."

This was important. He was not telling them that they had to join our union, just not to be afraid of the union. You see, many Portuguese immigrants had lived under António de Oliveira Salazar, prime minister of Portugal from 1932 to 1968, a rigid authoritarian who despised communism and socialism, and by extension, trade unions. In fact, he was the reason many Portuguese workingmen fled their native land for a better life in Canada, and many of these men had little experience of democracy, let alone labour organization. Most were afraid to join a union. Aceto's endorsement would clear that hurdle.

"I will send my organizers to your yard," I said, it being the place where all the men would assemble before going to various projects. "Just let them in and tell your superintendent to get lost for a while."

"Tomorrow morning?" Luigi asked me, which caught me by surprise because I was not ready to roll yet.

"No, no, the morning after," I replied. It was late at night and I would not be able to get anyone down there on time.

After that it was easy. We signed up almost all of the crews and we were subsequently certified by the OLRB. I brought that certificate to Lenny and he kept his word. Early in 1974, we started negotiations and by the spring of 1974, after my return from Harvard, we were able to reach an industry-wide agreement which was five cents an hour below the high-rise forming rate but double the average hourly rate of the house basement workers, meaning we added another eight hundred members to Local 183.

Lenny's company had, among his many crews, two that were composed entirely of hard-working Jamaicans. One of the Jamaicans, whom we used to call Brother Brown (Brown was his last name), served on a number of House Basement Negotiating Committees. He was always in a good humour and I enjoyed chatting with him during breaks in bargaining sessions. His life's dream was to save enough money to build a motel in Jamaica and retire there. He told me that I had a standing invitation to be his guest at any time. He also ran for election as a Local 183 executive board member. His campaign literature read: "Don't vote for black—vote for Brown"!

One time Lenny fired an employee from one of his Jamaican crews for allegedly making physical threats and running after his foreman with an axe. We took the matter to the OLRB and, understandably, Lenny was not pleased. He felt he was fully justified in discharging the employee for such a serious offence. The employee in question admitted on the stand that he had, in fact, run after the foreman with an axe. "But I did not hurt him," he said in his own defence. When asked why, he replied: "Because he ran faster than me."

Due to the brilliant defence advanced by the lawyer who represented us, Bernie Fishbein, now the chairman of the OLRB, we won the case. You can imagine Lenny's screams when he learned that not only did he have to reinstate the employee who ran after his foreman with an axe but he also had to pay him for time lost. I took Lenny to lunch and, as he was a gentleman and a progressive employer, he calmed down and did not appeal the case. Lenny continued to be fair with us and he was the lead representative of the house basement contractors' associations during future negotiations.

With our increased membership, it became almost impossible to operate from our St. Clair Avenue offices. We looked for a place to build a new office suitable for our expanded operations and bought an empty lot on the north side of Dupont Street just east of Dufferin. We engaged an architect, got a building permit, and called for tenders. The low bidder was Dineen Construction, a good union company. The sod-turning ceremony took place on May 15, 1974, and by Christmas we were operating from this new facility. It would take that long today just to get the paperwork processed.

The new three-storey building was 16,500 square feet with a meeting hall able to accommodate more than three hundred members. To us it was a palace and we were proud of it. Not in our wildest dreams could we have imagined that we would need a much bigger building in just a few more years.

As soon as we moved into our new building we computerized our office operations. I was prompted to adopt this new technology due to the fact that at the end of each month, the office staff went into a panic to report the per capita tax to the International. With our constant increase in membership it became a real challenge to comply on time. We were among the first, if not the first, Canadian labour union to install a computer system. In those days, computers were just beginning to be used. At first we engaged a British company known as Basic Four but it went bankrupt shortly thereafter, delaying our computing program for a few months. Not all our office staff were thrilled about this innovation. Some of them continued for a few years to use their old typewriters. In those days such resistance was quite common. Eventually many other union locals followed our example.

* * *

In 1975, the Italian government called the first conference for Italian immigrants spread around the globe. I was invited to participate as a delegate from an Italian-founded trade union, although I knew very little about unions in Italy. While I was there, I was approached by a functionary of the Italian consulate in Toronto, whom I knew. He asked me to assist the son of a friend in immigrating to Canada. His friend was Luigi (Gigi) Sturam, the director of the Post and Telegraph Office of the Italian Chamber of Deputies. This was a prestigious position, giving him access to many high-powered people in Italy. At that time, there was no Internet or e-mail. Members of Parliament in Rome had to rely on his office for communication. I said I knew very little about how to go about it but with me was another delegate from Toronto, Lorenzo Petricone, a sewer and water-main contractor who overheard the conversation. "Don't worry," he said. "I think I can help you."

Petricone was also an immigration consultant for the Italian government, an unpaid position. Italy used to have a number of so-called consultants around the world and they were pulled back to Rome a few times a year to report on the conditions of Italian emigrants. Petricone had forged a good friendship with the Canadian immigration offices in Rome and, in particular, with the woman in charge, so he did the standard Italian thing and arranged a lunch date. The woman in charge was a second-generation Italian from Quebec and she told us about Ottawa's restrictive policy regarding prospective Italian immigrants to Canada. The bottom line, her office had been told, verbally, so as not to leave a paper trail, was that it should grant visas to as few people as possible. (I feel a bit uneasy about disclosing what was definitely a confidential discussion but after fifty years I believe I can be forgiven for bringing it to light.) I could not believe her. Italian immigrants were nation builders. We had brought so much, contributed so much to Canada, and now to be rejected? It was too much.

Such is the nature of politics. On the one hand, Prime Minister Pierre Elliott Trudeau was pushing a multicultural policy and encouraging immigration to Canada, but on the other hand, he was breaking away from traditional sources of immigration in Western Europe. While his government maintained that the new policy was all about fairness, it had a clear political dimension. It served to smooth feathers ruffled by other issues such as the enforced policy of bilingualism. The multicultural policy was, in my opinion, a clever idea. It encouraged Anglophone Canada to support ethnic groups yet at the same time it maintained the solid support of Francophones who were the most resistant to erosion of their culture especially by so-called "allophones," those who spoke neither English nor French. Multiculturalism also provided the party in power with the opportunity to use taxpayer money to give generously and often to ethnic festivals, newspapers, folk-dance troupes, and similar organizations to curry favour and buy votes.

Most Italians in Canada believed, and some still do, that new-found prosperity in Italy negated emigration, and Trudeau was quite popular in the Italian community. But that masks the real reason why Italian immigration to Canada fell. The rule changes brought in by Trudeau made it much more difficult for Italians or any European immigrants to be welcomed in Canada. The new rules required a prospective immigrant to have a good knowledge of one of the two official languages and a degree from a recognized university. Quite simply, they put the bar so high that most Italians did not qualify to immigrate to Canada, even those with university degrees, because those degrees were often not recognized. In his book, *The Truth About Trudeau*, Bob Plamondon outlines the reality of Trudeau's immigration poli-cies. There were 183,974 immigrants to Canada in 1968 when he took power, representing about 1 per cent of the population. By 1984, that number was down to 0.3 per cent of the population. Also, Plamondon notes, 87 per cent of immigrants in the 1960s were of European origin. By 1979, Europe supplied a mere 30 per cent with the rest coming from Asia. The year before Trudeau's immigration law, 16,400 Italians arrived in Canada. The follow-ing year, eight hundred came, and by 1978 only two received an immigration visa.

Why was this? I think it was simply to protect the French language in Quebec. There were too many Italians in the province and the Italian language was widely used in commerce. I remem-ber in the late 1960s buying an Ontario lottery ticket where the rules were explained in English and Italian. In Quebec, Italian immigrants refused to send their children to French school as demanded by the Quebec government.

There was a mini-revolt over the school issue in a suburb of Montreal heavy with Italian immigrants. It is recorded as the Battle of Saint Léonard. Forty per cent of the population were of Italian heritage and most sent their kids to English schools. Francophones, fearing their culture and language would be shoved aside, pushed for and got the school board to adopt a policy requiring all incoming elementary school students in September 1968 to enrol in a French school, regardless of parental wishes. This caused no end of upset among the Italians who resorted to setting up secret schools in their homes. A grassroots movement organized private schools that began operating in former French schools that were now under-utilized. The dissension spread across Montreal with other English-rights groups taking up the cause. Both French and English militants objected and there were protests in the street. Despite attempts to legislate an end to the dispute, it dragged on until 1977 when René Lévesque's Parti Québécois government imposed French as the language of education under Bill 101. To this day, resentment lingers.

This subtle discrimination against Italians is ongoing. In 2002, a young Italian mechanical engineer paid good money to study English at York University. He was the best in his class. He also attended a computer engineering program at a Jewish Vocational School, again paying good money. Although he was one of the youngest in the class, he was such a good student his instructor offered him a position as a teacher's assistant. Upon his return to Italy he applied to immigrate to Canada. Three years later, the Canadian Embassy in Rome rejected his application on the grounds that his command of the English language was insufficient. They did this without even speaking to him. Sure, they gave him points for his education and job experience but they scored him low enough in language to ensure he did not qualify.

The irony is that while the young man was waiting for his visa in Italy, he was transferred by his employer, a multinational corporation, to Thailand where he became the sales manager for their operations in the Far East, including Japan, Australia, New Zealand, Vietnam, and Burma, mostly because of his ability to speak English. Yet he was not good enough for Canada. He was later promoted to vice-president of his company.

Going back to our lunch in Rome, our immigration contact at the Canadian Embassy promised to help and that son of a friend of a friend was allowed into Canada. As the son of a high-ranking Italian civil servant, well-educated with a degree in economics, he could have landed a great job in Italy. He emigrated because he wanted a different life. I was happy for him.

The conference in Rome was attended by more than 1,000 delegates representing Italian emigrants from all over the world. It was held at the headquarters of the Food and Agricultural Organization of the United Nations. Speaker after speaker, mostly Italian politicians, talked at length of concern for "our workers overseas." I got fed up with this patronization and when I went to the podium emphasized that "our workers overseas" were Italians who had chosen to emigrate and that their problems were the concern of each of their chosen nations and, in our case, the Canadian trade union movement. I do not know if they were just being polite but I got loud applause from the delegates.

I mention all of this background because Trudeau's new immigration policies had a profound effect on Local 183. With Italian immigration blocked, the demand for workers was filled by illegal immigrants, primarily Portuguese. Regardless, they came to work even if they came illegally. It was easy to get around the immigration policies at that time and they were well instructed on how to jump the line by unscrupulous immigration consultants. The Portuguese were and are very good workers and vital to the construction industry and, in turn, to the Canadian and Ontario economies. Without them, the residential construction industry would have suffered greatly for lack of manpower. That holds true today and it is an issue I will delve into later.

CHAPTER 21

"THAT SON OF A BITCH!"

Having established a beachhead in the housing construction sector, Local 183 branched out into the residential concrete and drain sector starting around 1972. The concrete and drain industry is unique to the Greater Toronto Area. In other parts of Canada, this type of work is done by different contractors. It consists of laying both sanitary and storm sewer pipes within the basement excavation and then connecting them to the main municipal sewer and storm line on the street. In addition, the concrete and drain contractor sprays the gravel on both basements and garages, installs the wire mesh, and pours concrete on top as well as making any concrete steps the house may require.

Our first approach to this sector was to organize the high-rise concrete and drain industry. Within a short time, it was fully signed up, although the truth is there were only a hundred concrete and drain workers in the high-rise sector. From 1976 to 1978, we began in earnest to organize the concrete and drain contractors in low-rise housing where the majority were employed. It was a slow process. The majority of contractors were small with a strong influence on their employees. I used my usual strategy, sending organizers into the field to make personal contact with the owners. In each case we spread the union gospel: to the workers, the benefit of being represented by a union; to the contractor, the benefit of stability and fair competition. And it worked. One of our newer representatives, Tony Dionisio, was particularly active in this campaign and we added another eight hundred members to Local 183.

Not everything went smoothly in all sectors as we grew. In the spring of 1976, we were renewing our civil engineering collective agreements and one of them was the utilities contract, which involved cable installation, mainly underground, and primarily for Bell Telephone. There were about a dozen contractors working this sector and the largest was G. M. Guest which employed some four or five hundred of our members and had about an 80 per cent market share. As usual, I met informally with the company manager. We had reached an off-the-record understanding on an amount we thought was reasonable for both parties. Just before the official meeting at which time the Utility Contractors Association was expected to table its final proposal, the manager called me in for a coffee. He told me that contrary to his recommendations, the company's parent in Montreal, Atlas Corporation, had vetoed the amount we had agreed on and instructed him to table a lower offer. I told him this was not acceptable and he advised me to go on strike because, in his opinion, the head office folks would probably agree to the original deal after a few days of work stoppage.

He did not have to advise me on a strike. Our members were chomping at the bit to strike. We called a special membership meeting where the last official employers' proposal was rejected and a strike was duly called. A week later, the manager again called me for coffee and again, off-the-record, told me head office were digging their heels in and wanted to table an even a smaller increase. So we just continued the strike and kept the pickets up. Normally in a strike like this, members start approaching me after the fourth week and asking when I think things will be settled. It is not that they want to get back to work so much as their wives are pestering them with a daily "honey-do" list. Some would complain of being "pushed" by their wives to do major work around the house. They worked harder on strike than when they were on the job.

A new offer did come in around the fourth week but now the members were angry at being forced to strike and they over-whelmingly rejected it. It took seven weeks before the Contractors' Association tabled a more generous proposal, one that was more than we had expected. A secret vote of the negotiating committee was taken and much to my surprise it carried by only a few votes. A year later, I was speaking to the chairman of the negotiating committee, a man I respected for his common sense.

"Verne, that was a very strange strike last year."

"If it was not for me we would still be on strike," he confided.

"Why?" I asked.

He responded: "When the committee was counting the votes, I was tabulating the result. I announced at the meeting the 'Yes' vote but used the numbers of the 'No' votes and vice versa. The settlement was too good to be turned down!"

I was shocked. I did not know what to do. On reflection, I decided it was too late to turn back the clock. The collective agreement was signed and, according to the law, both parties had to agree for it to be reopened. It would have been too embarrassing for all concerned.

* * *

I wish all of our contracts were open-and-shut cases but they never were, and never are; even when you think it should be easy it isn't, and other times, when you are expecting a fight, sometimes it never comes. For example, in 1979 we renewed our collective agreements with the high-rise residential sector and ran into an unexpected and unusual dispute. At first, our talks with the Metropolitan Toronto Apartment Builders Association went smoothly. We reached a tentative agreement with the negotiating committee for a $1.72 increase an hour over two years. Their negotiating committee included my old friend Harold Green of Greenwin, acting as chairman, Bev Howard from Meridian, and Bill Mascoll from Belmont Construction.

A few days after the signing the memorandum of understanding I got a call from Green: "Call a strike!"

Now, this is something I usually hear from the union side of the table, not from the owners' spokesman, so I was a little surprised. Harold was furious and meant every word, saying all the players had bailed on the deal: "Those avaricious pigs turned down our settlement! Bill Mascoll double-crossed us! Rather than recommending the settlement to our association he spoke against it."

I assured Harold that, given the circumstances, his advice was superfluous. We were in a legal position to strike and strike we would. Mind you, I did like talking with Harold because he was quite the wordsmith. He would have been about fifty years old then and was taking English literature and composition classes at university. He quite often corrected me, for example, when I described the cost of a product as "cheap."

"Don't use that word," he lectured, "say 'economical,' because 'cheap' suggests poor quality."

Both Harold and I saw Bill Mascoll's behaviour as despicable. When you negotiate, you must act in good faith and with integrity. You cannot agree to something at the table, sign off on it, and then turn around and shoot it down. It is dishonest. Having signed the agreement, he was bound to convince his colleagues at the association to ratify it. The strike was called and we went back to the table. In the interim, Harold was fired and replaced by Joe Bergman, from Cadillac Fairview, the entity which had been created in 1974 by the merger of Cadillac Development Corporation and Fairview Corporation. Joe had founded Cadillac Development with Eph Diamond and Jack Kamin in 1953 while Fairview was part of the Bronfman family empire.

About a week into the strike, the Ministry of Labour called a meeting between the parties which, at our request, was held in our union office on Dupont Street. We prepared carefully, setting up a U-shaped table in an empty office space. The mediation officer would sit at the apex of the U and each side would look across the gap between the tables in front of him.

I had a plan and I told Reilly to be ready for the cue which was the question from their side of the table: "Who is he?"

He was puzzled but I told him just to do what I asked. When the cue came he was to jump in and jab his finger at Bill Mascoll and say: "That son of a bitch!"

"Don't worry," I said. "It's going to play out just like that."

I also told my secretary to come up to the second floor about half an hour after the start of the meeting to tell Joe Bergman that there was a call for him. When he came down she was to say that the person must have hung up.

So as we started the meeting I emphasized the principle of bargaining in good faith, which is not only required by law but is fundamental in every bargaining procedure. As the mediation officer nodded his head, I also said we cannot carry on with negotiation unless a person from the other side that betrayed this principle is removed, restoring integrity to the table.

Joe Bergman, who was not experienced in labour negotiation, immediately responded as I knew he would: "Who is he?"

Reilly played his part perfectly. As soon as the cue was triggered, he pointed his finger at Mascoll and said: "That son of a bitch!"

Boom. Mascoll was removed from their committee. A little later, my secretary, right on cue, came up to tell Joe Bergman there was a call for him. I went downstairs with him where, of course, he was told the other party must have hung up. We turned around but, just as I had expected, this ruse gave us few moments alone and Joe took the initiative to open up.

"Look, the settlement Harold reached was too rich for us, we have to come up with a lower one."

"Joe," I said, shaking my head. "That was before the strike. Now it will cost more."

After a brief silence, Joe asked me: "How much?"

"It'll be $1.85 and I'm doing you a favour."

Actually we were doing ourselves a favour. The number was a compromise. I realized that the higher the hourly rate, the fewer the number of labourers that would end up working for the builders. The builders would quite simply make each trade—carpenters, plumbers, drywallers, and electricians—do their own cleanup. We signed the new memorandum of settlement that same day in our lawyer's office. The ink was not even dry when I got a call from Harold screaming at me over the phone because the new settlement was higher than the $1.72-an-hour increase we had previously agreed.

"Harold," I replied. "It was out of respect for you we settled so low. We could have got a lot more!"

There was silence on the other end of the phone, then I heard a loud laugh.

"You, too, are a son of a bitch . . . but a nice one!"

He then invited me for dinner at Carmen's Club restaurant on Alexander Street where we enjoyed a good bottle of wine and a juicy steak, sharing some war stories and some laughs. The real surprise came a week later. Joe Bergman invited me for a cup of coffee at a Merton Street restaurant.

"When you called the strike you hit my soft spot," he said, and there were genuine tears in his eyes. "I still remember the days when we were hungry, when my parents were on strike in Winnipeg."

I will never forget that moment. I wanted to hug Joe in solidarity because no one wants a strike. It disrupts families and it is emotionally difficult. Our guys want to work and they take pride in their jobs. It is how they support their families and build their lives. It is the union weapon of last resort and I think Joe understood that better than most, from personal experience.

Green remained the spokesman for the apartment builders except for one period in the 1980s, although he remained on the committee. We were a tight group, even though we represented different interests. It was a tradition for all parties to meet informally before negotiations. One year, about a week before the high-rise contract talks with the builders, we had one of our informal dinners at the Katsura Japanese restaurant in the Prince Hotel on York Mills Road. During dinner I was presented with the builders' position by the Belmont representative who was acting as chairman and given some lengthy explanations as to why they were taking their stance.

I turned around and shot down their proposals, one by one. Green, who was not leading the committee but was still on it, was enjoying every moment but before things got out of hand he stepped in and intervened to protect their interests. When Harold stepped up, things settled down and another settlement was reached. Sometimes it really is about knowing the players and being reasonable.

CHAPTER 22

LESSONS IN NEGOTIATION

Negotiations are like a game of chess. No two games are alike. Every move is important. At the negotiating table there is jockeying for position, sometimes for the benefit of the audience of either side. The real negotiations and the most productive are those off-the-record conversations, when both parties meet at a golf course or break bread together without fear of being quoted. In this setting, people open up to each other and most of the time they seek common ground. I became an expert at this and endured a multitude of breakfasts, lunches, and dinners to meet key employers in each sector to explore common ground. My tactics were simple. I would try to get each key employer to give a number of concessions I could assemble at the negotiating table into an overall package.

At the same time, I would do my homework. I would talk to a number of my own members who I thought would reflect the view of the majority. I never asked a direct question such as "What would it take to settle?" but rather asked something like "Assuming the employers propose this, what do you think?"

During my thirty-two years of union work, I never signed a memorandum of settlement that was rejected by the members in a secret ballot because I always did my homework.

In the spring of 1978 I faced a new reality. No employer wanted to meet me off the record. In addition, the four contractor associations—roads, sewers, heavy construction, and utility—had bonded together and formed a common front, guided by the very able lawyer Stan Dinsdale. Stan had figured out my modus operandi and put a stop to it. As I have said, nobody wants to strike over a relatively small difference but in this case we were close to a strike and still far apart. I knew our only chance was to get an off-the-record conversation going because we did not want a weak settlement or a prolonged strike but if something did not change we were going to end up there.

In my own mind, I tried to visualize the overall strategic situation. I analyzed the so-called enemy front of the four associations, united and consolidated against us. My first task would be to break that common front. My analysis led me to the Sewer and Water-Main Association as the weakest link, and in particular one company, Con Drain, which represented 40 per cent of the sector. Fred De Gasperis and his brothers had founded the company. He was an extremely intelligent man who came here, like so many from Italy, as an eighteen-year-old and found work digging trenches. He built a business and became one of the richest men in Canada.

I knew Fred fairly well. He was a good employer who never forgot his roots. I had to talk to him and I also knew Fred was associated with Marco Muzzo, another extraordinary person and also a legend in land development. My friend Primo Di Luca was close to Marco and they had worked together to rebuild three villages destroyed in the terrible earthquake in my home area of Friuli in 1976, which killed 939 people, injured 2,400, and left 157,000 homeless. Primo received the Order of Canada for his work on the reconstruction committee and he was my best man at my wedding and godfather to my son, Mark. So on a Saturday morning, about a week before the strike deadline, I went to Primo's house.

"Primo, please call your friend Marco and ask him to set up a meeting between me and Freddy," I asked.

The next morning, Sunday, Primo duly called me: "Freddy will be waiting for you today at 2 p.m. in his office."

I went and met with him and found he had taken time off from a family confirmation celebration at his company yard on Connie Street. This was a great mark of respect to me so I came directly to the point. I put forward our rock-bottom position and said: "Freddy, nobody wants a strike. It is not in the interest of anybody but if I put forward this position officially they would try to squeeze me down further."

Freddy listened carefully and at the end, said: "Fine, I will go along with this and the other conditions but I want my three hours back."

What he was referring to were the three hours of work which had been reduced from the work week, taking it to forty-five hours a week from the forty-eight hours in the last contract. This provision was not in effect yet because it was due to be implemented on the last day of the collective agreement. This was an important issue to me and historically for the trade union movement. The first recorded strike in history was during the construction of the pyramids when workers went on strike to have one day off a week. May 1 was International Labour Day, celebrated in memory of those shot by the police during the famous slaughterhouse strike in Chicago in 1886. They had been striking for an eight-hour day. I was also hesitant to give up those three hours because we had paid for them. When we negotiated the previous agreement the federal Anti-Inflation Board was in effect. It had been instituted by the Trudeau government to control wages and prices. It succeeded in controlling wages but not prices and in our case the AIB forced us to reduce our increase by thirty-five cents per hour (which at that time was good money) with the strange rationale that a decrease in the hours of work corresponded in higher earning by overtime pay. This bore no relation to reality because no contractor pays overtime unless forced by circumstances outside his control.

Freddy was adamant, however. "Our industry," he said, "is subject to weather conditions. Sometimes we cannot work because it is too cold. Sometime it is too hot. Other times it is raining and during the spring thaw it is muddy. We have invested millions in equipment. The nature of the job has changed and your labourers are not doing the heavy jobs they did in the past. Today it is done by machinery. The Operating Engineers have already renewed this agreement with us for a forty-eight-hour week and they would have accepted fifty hours if we had proposed it to them." I thought about this for a while and realized keeping the status quo around the work week was the lesser of the evils. I agreed and we shook hands.

"I will go to our association," Freddy said. "If they don't sign for that amount I will." That meant the others would follow and the domino effect would prompt the other three associations to follow suit.

On Thursday of that week, the conciliation officers of the Ministry of Labour called us for another meeting, on Friday morning. As we were entering the elevator of the MOL building on University Avenue, one of the paving contractor negotiators turned to me and said: "I don't understand what is going on. Yesterday we were marching in one direction, today the opposite!"

Nothing much happened during the day as the conciliation officer went from committee to committee and the four associations reviewed and discussed a new proposal they were to submit to us. We spent the entire night either playing cards or sleeping on the desks. Early Saturday morning, we were presented with a new proposal and, no surprise, it was what Freddy and I had agreed upon. The proposed increases and conditions were ratified by secret ballot and later I learned what the contractors had been up to. They had tried all day and night to convince Freddy not to go alone but he stuck by his commitment to me. In the end, they gave in and a fair settlement was reached and a strike was averted. Years later, Fred pulled me aside and said: "You know that even today my wife does not believe that I spent that night with you over this!"

* * *

Little by little, we had grown Local 183 from a small labourers' union into a serious player in the construction industry, representing many different sectors and many different skill sets. We were always on the lookout for a new sector to add and while sometimes it was obvious, other times it was just serendipity.

Case in point: the Industrial Division of Local 183. Early one morning back in the 1960s, we got a phone call from some plastic pool factory workers wanting to be organized. It was completely by chance because they had called other union offices early that morning but no one had answered. We just happened to be in the office at 7 a.m. and picked up the phone. The rest is history.

Similarly, after we organized the high-rise apartment builders we started getting calls from employees working at the builder's property management and maintenance crews. These included building superintendents, cleaners, grounds crews, and handymen. In 1975, we launched a full-on organizing campaign and brought hundreds of new members into our ranks from these sectors. The negotiations were often difficult. Building superintendents, for instance, had to be grouped into different pay scale brackets, reflecting the number of units they managed in their building. Again we were helped by Harold Green, whose property management company had the largest number of residential units. The majority of the members in the Industrial Department were office cleaners. It started with Hurley Brothers and expanded to include Lester B. Pearson International Airport terminal workers.

The largest factory we organized was Burlington Carpet in Brampton which at one point employed more than eight hundred of our members. This multinational had eight mills in North America and the Brampton Mill was the only one organized. Our efforts made quite an impression on the International. Once when we were on strike, the general secretary, Arthur E. Coia, joined me on the picket line to boost morale. It was a busy unit and the chief steward, a Jamaican man, was almost full-time on our payroll because he spent so much of his day helping members with their various and many grievances. It all ended when Canadian Prime Minister Brian Mulroney signed a free trade agreement with the United States and the multinational closed down the Brampton plant and moved its operations to non-union mills in the United States.

When I left Local 183 in 1992 there were approximately 2,000 members in the Industrial Division. Not all the members we brought in stayed with Local 183, however. By 1976, we represented a lot of cement finishers working in heavy construction and residential high-rise concrete forming. I was approached by Brian Yandell, the business manager of Operative Plasterers and Cement Mason International Association Local 598, to see if we were interested in a merger with his members. Local 598 represented about five hundred steeplejacks and cement finishers working in the ICI (Industrial Commercial Institutional) sector and for four sidewalk contractors. Needless to say, I was interested. Brian invited me to speak to his membership but warned me there was a militant group among the steeplejacks who would be opposed to any change and it could get violent.

I brought two members with me, Paddy Burns and Tom O'Neil, two true fighting Irishmen. Neither man looked for trouble but if provoked, they would clean up the provocateurs. Paddy, in particular, was strong as a bull, not too tall but afraid of nothing. Both had good hearts and when I asked them to join me and explained why I needed their help, they stepped up immediately. The meeting went fairly smoothly maybe because both Paddy and Tommy were with me on the stage. I explained the advantages of joining our union, paying particular attention to the services and benefits we provided. Within a few months we had certified the four sidewalk companies and six cement finishing contractors, representing about 90 per cent of the industry, but none of the steeplejacks.

Nevertheless, we moved ahead and hired Yandell and his secretary. The cement finishing contractors mounted a strong opposition to our application for certification at the Labour Board and the case dragged on for six months. Eventually, in 1977, we negotiated our first contract in this sector.

A couple of years after, the cement finishers went to Local 506. They had a newly elected manager in the person of Mike Gargaro. He had complained constantly that the ICI sector was the jurisdiction of Local 506 and that cement finishers should be part of Local 506. We agreed to go along for two reasons: first, Arthur E. Coia, the International general secretary treasurer appealed to us to go along and we respected him; second, we wanted to get along with Local 506 and Gargaro. Unfortunately, our good faith gesture did not pay off with Gargaro, as we will see later. Quite the reverse. It only increased his appetite for more of the fruits of our labours.

CHAPTER 23

SNAPPED AT BY TRUDEAU

Everyone knows it takes money for a politician to campaign and get enough votes to be elected. I do not say this in any derogatory way but just to note that it is the practical part of a democratic process. It is no secret Local 183 gave a monthly contribution to the Ontario New Democratic Party (NDP) and was the only construction union to do so. From time to time we also financially supported individual candidates at all levels of government whom we thought would support our cause. We also bought tickets to fundraising events and dinners. Of course, we pushed our viewpoint at every opportunity, sometimes with success and sometimes not so successfully.

As a union we were big believers in democracy and politics. We always preached how important it is to vote. Gallagher emphasized this at every meeting and I followed his lead. To vote, of course, you have to be a citizen so we also pushed members to become Canadian citizens, setting up a program to help them through the process. We helped more than two hundred people within a few weeks, 172 of whom obtained citizenship.

I think it was one of the most important programs Local 183 undertook.

One morning in 1977, while drinking my coffee, I read in the newspaper that the government of Canada had struck a parliamentary committee to review the citizenship laws and were asking interested parties to make submissions. That same day, I formed a small committee to prepare a brief and asked our lawyer, Ray Koskie, to assist. We wanted to make our point that it was in the best interest of Canada to lower the waiting period for becoming a citizen to three years from five. The brief was well received by the parliamentary committee. In their opinion, it was the best brief they had seen. In due time, the law was changed and the waiting period was lowered. We do not claim the credit for this change but certainly we had some influence.

I did not have much opportunity to bend the ear of all our prime ministers but sometime towards the end of the 1970s I did cross words with one memorable politician, Pierre Elliott Trudeau, who was prime minister from 1968 to 1979 and again from 1980 to 1984. I got a call from the Prime Minister's Office in Ottawa inviting me to a dinner with Trudeau on his next visit to Toronto in the small private basement room of an Italian restaurant on Wilson Avenue. There were several members of the Italian community among the dozen or so guests and the Prime Minister's assistant and another three MPs, including my friend Charles Caccia.

We were seated around a square table during dinner and afterwards Trudeau gave a speech declaring that "the country's unity" was the most important national issue of the time. Indeed, the Parti Québécois, under René Lévesque, had won the election in Quebec in 1976 and was aggressively pushing to separate from Canada. Lévesque had brought in Bill 101 to make French the common language of the province. The federal government and the PQ would face off in the 1980 referendum which was held to determine whether Québec would leave the confederation. As it turned out, some 60 per cent of voters rejected separation.

Although separatism was the news of the moment, I was more interested in other matters. In the world I was coming from, it was more important to talk about jobs. In those days we had high unemployment in our sector, as much as 30 per cent, because the economy was struggling under high interest rates. When I was asked to speak at the Trudeau dinner I said I felt the country's main problem was the economy, given our high unemployment rate. Trudeau interrupted me and said: "You sound like the Leader of the Opposition."

I was not following federal politics that closely and I did not even know what the Leader of the Opposition, Joe Clark, was saying and so I replied: "With all due respect, I do not know what the Leader of the Opposition is saying, but I know what our members are saying to me."

Trudeau snapped back: "It is not the government's role to give a job to every Canadian."

Before I could answer him, the Prime Minister turned away and let somebody else talk. Later, he came back to me, asking: "What would you do to stimulate the economy?"

"I would lower the mortgage rate on houses," I said, "given that every job created in this kind of construction creates another four in other sectors of the economy."

At that time the mortgage rate was 12 per cent or more and rising. The construction industry is a barometer of any country's economy and the higher the interest rates climbed, the more pain we felt and the more unemployment grew. Mortgage rates peaked at 18 per cent in 1981.

Trudeau snarled: "It's not the federal government's job to provide a home for every Canadian but we're already doing something in this sense."

He was referring to a federal program to offset the cost of insulating houses to make them more energy efficient. Unfortunately, this program was not delivering much in terms of employment in the construction industry. It was like giving an aspirin to somebody who was seriously sick. Trudeau did not allow me to speak anymore. The other guests were anxious to acclaim him, perhaps with the hope of getting some important appointment.

As we left the restaurant my friend Charles Caccia said to me in Italian: "You did well to underline the state of the economy. We, too, try to tell him the same thing but he doesn't listen to us." It was the last time I received an invitation from Trudeau.

On the other hand, I had a cordial and fruitful relationship with another politician, the Honourable Bill Davis, Progressive Conservative leader and Premier of Ontario from 1971 to 1985. You would think a conservative politician and a union leader would be toe to toe but I have to say Davis was a pleasure to meet and work with. He taught me a valuable lesson about respect. I cannot remember exactly when I was asked to meet with him at his Queen's Park office. In those days, I was a typical Roman Italian in that I was late for almost everything. It was nothing personal. It was just part of my culture. On this day, I showed up twenty minutes late to meet the Premier. Davis did not appear to be mad at me but he sat there puffing on his pipe for a couple of minutes while the meeting got started. He then leaned in and said in that trademark calm voice of his: "You know, it's not right to be late for meetings. It's really a sign of disrespect. People should always show respect by being punctual. You should make being on time part of your plan."

I thought about it and I realized he was right. His words left a lasting impression on me and from that day forward I was always not only on time but sometimes early. A few years later I was on a flight back from a meeting in Florida and the weather was so awful around Toronto that they diverted the aircraft to Montreal. The following day, early on a Sunday morning we took another flight back to Toronto. As I entered the arrivals lounge I looked up and saw Premier Bill Davis standing there, smiling. I was surprised, of course, but he recognized me and shook my hand and laughed.

"Must be nice to have business in Florida this time of year, John," he said.

"How did you know I was in Florida?" I asked.

"Because my wife was on the same flight which was diverted from Toronto and I'm here to pick her up!"

I wish I could have stayed longer and chatted with him but I was really pressed for time. I had to rush back to Toronto for our regular monthly membership meeting that Sunday morning. I rarely missed them. Davis empathized with my plight and graciously asked me to extend his greetings to the members and his respect "for such hard-working people." Bill Davis was a great politician and a good friend, as much as he could be, to LIUNA 183 and the labour movement.

CHAPTER 24

MY ESTABLISHMENT YEARS

On August 18, 1975, Michael Starr, chairman of the Workmen's Compensation Board, as it was then called, appointed me to the newly established Joint Consultative Committee. This committee was made up of two labour representatives, two employer representatives, two from the WCB, and two from the public at large. The other labour committee member was the safety director of the Ontario Federation of Labour. The committee's role was to comment on proposed changes to the Workmen's Compensation Act of Ontario and the administration of the Workmen's Compensation Board. Later on, we initiated our own proposals. It was a very useful experience and I think we made a substantial contribution to WCB policies and procedures as well as changes to the Act.

They were not earth-shattering amendments but very useful to injured workers. At the time, the big issue was that the process discriminated against injured workers. In fact, the year before, injured workers had formed the Union of Injured Workers (UIW) to highlight their cause with the government and the WCB. The key issue was the definition of pensions for permanent partial disabilities caused on the job. We were sympathetic to injured workers but one of the problems we were unable to sort out was back injuries, a constant problem, especially in construction.

I would resign from this committee in September 1983 because of various other commitments but it gave me great insight into the political hierarchy. I was also gaining visibility myself at the top levels of the Ontario labour scene and one evening in 1977, while playing cards in my office, I got a call from Dr. Bette Stephenson, then the Ontario Minister of Labour. She called on my private line, a number known to very few people. Even fewer people would have known I would be at the office at 9 p.m. playing cards, although it was something we did from time to time during the snowy months.

I set up my desk like a kitchen table because I did not want members or other visitors sitting across a desk and feeling uncomfortable or intimidated. A kitchen table desk was more informal and made the atmosphere more familiar especially for Italians who like to discuss problems around their own kitchen tables. It was also good for playing cards!

I was curious when I realized it was Dr. Stephenson on the line and even more curious to know why she was calling.

"John," she said, "I want you to be a controller on the Workmen's Compensation Board, and I don't want no for an answer!"

I was surprised at both the time of the call and the subject matter. The job was a full-time, high-level government job with higher pay and good security. Also, my Local 183 job always depended on me being re-elected. It was tempting. I thanked her and said I would think about it. She seemed a bit disappointed that I did not give her an immediate yes.

I did think long and hard about the offer but declined for a number of reasons. I felt my union building was just beginning and I was not thrilled at the idea of losing my freedom of movement and being tied to an office job. There were other reasons but it mostly did not feel like my true destiny. Dr. Stephenson was a good Minister of Labour and I would have been proud to serve her. She improved safety legislation and in particular she strengthened the right of an employee to refuse unsafe work. Her colleague Dr. Bob Elgie was also a good Minister of Labour. I managed to embarrass myself when I was sitting at the table with him during a union Christmas dinner and blurted out: "Finally, we have a minister who is not a lawyer!" He looked at me sternly and replied: "But I am also a lawyer!" I should note that there was another Liberal Minister of Labour who had been appointed by the David Peterson government in 1987 who was very good to work with: Greg Sorbara. He later became Ontario Minister of Finance.

Still, as I mulled over Dr. Stephenson's call, I reminded myself that I had not enjoyed my experiences with government agencies. Premier Bill Davis had appointed me as a director of the Ontario Housing Corporation (OHC), at that time the second largest landlord in North America after New York's Public Housing Authority. It was terrible. There were usually monthly meetings, sometimes twice a month, lasting a whole afternoon and into the night. The weekend before each meeting, a courier would deliver a couple of thick agendas. I had little free time before but with this appointment I had none at all. I made no real contribution to OHC, primarily because I just did not have the time to dedicate to the role in order to understand and analyze the many issues the board had to deal with.

* * *

My real job was running a large, growing, and diversified union local but there were always these pressures from either the government or the labour movement pulling me in different directions. It came to a head around 1979. We had a problem with the district council and I realized I was going to have to step up and put my leadership on the line, even if it meant moving away from Local 183, which was a painful choice. It was an issue of politics on many levels. The Laborers International Union's constitution consisted of three parts: the first applicable to the International per se, the second to an area district council, and the last to the locals. The district councils were created to coordinate and control certain activities of the locals in a geographical area, primarily a large metropolitan area such as Chicago or New York or part of a state. In 1969, the International chartered a district council for all locals in Ontario. The first manager was my friend Mike Reilly. He worked hard and tried to take over the negotiation of most agreements as per the district council's constitution. However, he met fierce resistance from most local managers, jealous of their independence. In early 1973, Reilly approached me, asking to come back to Local 183. "Look," he said, "I have a big family and cannot stay away for long and Ontario is a big province."

I welcomed him back with open arms and appointed him as my right-hand man. Others spread rumours that the real reason he quit was that he was not going to be re-elected but to me it did not matter why he quit, I was just glad that he was back with us. Taking Reilly's place was Henry Mancinelli, the manager of the Hamilton local. Mancinelli brought a different attitude. He promoted greater freedom among the locals. Over the years Henry and I became good friends and helped each other but in 1975, Henry also quit and went back to Hamilton.

This in itself was a problem. The district council is very important to our local. The union constitution gives it the power to negotiate and approve all local agreements. This makes sense in a metropolitan area like Toronto but less so across a province as diversified as Ontario, which is larger in land mass than either Texas or California. It makes the process more cumbersome and less democratic. There were other problems, too. There were tensions between Toronto and other parts of the province. Everybody elsewhere in Ontario hates Toronto, even though Toronto pays for most of the services they enjoy. We were also uncomfortable about how even though Local 183 represented 100 per cent of the members in certain collective agreements, such as with the apartment builders, we had only six votes out of fifty-six at the district council where agreements were ratified.

The deeper issue, however, was that Local 183 was the only local organized in the residential sector. There is a different mentality between the ICI (industrial, commercial, institutional) and the residential sectors. Like day and night. ICI unions are focused on a single trade. They are more rigid and deal primarily with general contractors. The residential union deals with multiple trades, and is flexible in dealing with family-owned contractors and home builders. The flexibility factor was always very important to me. My love of history and military strategy convinced me flexibility was the key to the success of many commanders on the battlefield. I could not and would not allow other interests to confine Local 183 to a straitjacket. So in 1975, I asked one of our representatives, Mike O'Brien, to run for the job and with the alliance of Ontario locals, he was elected as district council manager.

Unfortunately, by the next election, in 1979, it was evident he was not going to be re-elected. Political alliances had changed and there was a new manager at Local 506, Mike Gargaro. He resented the progress of Local 183 and wanted to claim back the residential sector. He tried to lure away two of my key assistant managers by offering them substantially higher pay but I cut him off thanks to a tip I got from one of my representatives.

Gargaro was no pushover. He skilfully united a number of Ontario locals in a common front against us and put forward his own candidate for district council manager, Ray Ford, the previous business manager of Local 506. Ray and I were good friends. We had attended the Canadian Labour College in 1963 together and when he became the manager of Local 506, the two of us tried to formulate a plan to amalgamate certain operations of the two locals, and eliminate duplication. The proposal was shot down at the executive board of Local 506 which, of course, was led by Gargaro, who later dethroned Ford and became the manager himself.

I then decided to throw my hat into the ring since O'Brien did not have a chance. I lost by two votes. However, Gargaro's games became more transparent and shortly afterwards the Sudbury local's four delegates left the Gargaro alliance and joined us, giving us a two-vote majority. The manager of the Sudbury local knew something was not right. In Chicago, during an international union conference, he was tapped by a small group of Ontario conspirators to frame me by putting drugs in my suitcase. The plot failed because they were too cheap to come up with the cash to buy the drugs and the manager, having seen how far they would go, wanted nothing to do with them and crossed over.

Our alliance dominated the bimonthly meetings of the district council and we were able to neutralize Gargaro's moves for a couple of years. In 1981, Ray Ford came to see me and said: "I am tired of doing Gargaro's bidding, I want to quit. You should be the manager of the council and I would like to be the administrator of the Provincial Training Fund."

Before he would quit, however, he wanted the backing of Arthur E. Coia, the chairman of the Provincial Training Fund which had been set up by the International. At first it might have seemed a risky strategy because Gargaro was so attached to Coia. Every time Arthur came to Toronto, Gargaro would pick him up at the airport with the local's Lincoln and chauffeur him around town, taking him to breakfast, lunch, and dinner. What Gargaro did not know was that Coia was a smart man and easily able to differentiate friendship from union business. I called Arthur, who was in Florida at a union meeting, and asked to meet.

"I can't come up now, but why don't you come down here," he said. "I can see you tomorrow night after a working dinner, say around 9:30 p.m."

He gave me the name of a hotel in Fort Lauderdale and asked me to be discreet. I asked O'Brien to come with me since I really do not like flying, especially alone, and we went to Florida the next day. Arthur was about an hour late. He apologized for the delay and listened intently to our story. I told him about Ford's intention and his request for Coia's support. Coia asked me if I wanted to be the manager of the district council.

"Yes, but I doubt the executive board will appoint me because out of seven votes, I have only one," I replied.

"Leave it to me," said Arthur. "I will take care of that."

The following week, Coia came to Toronto, and Ford resigned with a commitment from Coia who then met with the executive board of the district council. Three hours later, he came out and said: "The job is yours if you want it."

You have to understand I was in no mood to celebrate. I had to tender my resignation as business manager of Local 183 and it broke my heart. The local had meant everything to me. It had been the focus of all my energies and passion. I had grown so much with the organization, through all its ups and downs. I asked the local executive board to appoint Reilly to replace me and they did. The only thing Rita noticed was that the colour of my paycheque had changed.

"Did you change jobs?" she asked.

"It is all the same," I replied, though it was not really true. I did not want to worry her.

The first few months were hell. The district council executive board members, with the exception of one, were stacked against me. They attacked me personally at every turn and I almost quit to go back to Local 183. It occurred to me that my quitting was what they wanted. I stayed, and slowly their attitudes turned around. One of them, Rocco D'Andrea, the business manager from Sarnia, confided to me they had feared a return of Reilly's tactics and thought I was his agent. Only after they were fully convinced that I was my own man and that I was an asset to their locals did they open up and become loyal and true friends and staunch supporters. The exception was Gargaro.

I implemented two important programs for the locals. By increasing the per capita payment to the district council, mainly from Locals 183 and 506, we were able to pay for the locals' legal expenses, which in some cases were considerable in areas such as jurisdictional disputes with other unions. The second was to hire regional organizers to help the locals to organize non-union contractors. We also inserted clauses into collective agreements for the collection of working dues to be remitted to the district council.

Gargaro tried to sabotage my programs by diverting the new funds to his local and I was forced to take the matter to the Ontario Labour Relations Board. Coia even intervened to help Gargaro but he was not going to fight us at the district council. He asked me to withdraw the case and said that he would settle the matter and within a few weeks he sent Bob Connerton, the general counsel of the International, to meet with Gargaro and me.

"How much does Local 506 owe to the Council?" Bob asked. I gave him a number, which was actually twice the real figure, thinking that if they were going to shave it back, at least I would start high. Predictably, Gargaro complained it was too much.

"Okay, I recommend this amount," said Connerton, jotting down a figure, which was 75 per cent of my inflated starting point.

"I don't like it," I replied, feigning disappointment. "But in the interest of co-operation with the International, I reluctantly accept it." Gargaro had no choice but to go along, which meant the council got 25 per cent more than it was due.

In 1983, I ran for re-election to the district council and Gargaro ran one of his representatives, Tony Neil, a capable and well-respected man who had been a long-standing employee of the council. Tony won eight votes out of the fifty-six cast, those from his own local and a small industrial local whose manager was playing the parties against each other trying to leverage some benefit for himself. He picked the wrong horse. After that, no one ran against me and I won by acclamation each time.

CHAPTER 25

YOU CAN GO HOME AGAIN

I n the spring of 1983, Tony Lucas, a Portuguese union representative I had hired in the early 1970s, came to visit me at the
district council office. He said that if I was not going to return
to Local 183, he was going to run against Reilly in the upcoming spring election. It was for a four-year term and he said he
was running because he was unhappy with the way Reilly was
running the local and he felt he could do better. He said other
representatives felt the same way. Lucas was a good man, loyal
and hard-working, but I did not think he would be a suitable
manager for a complex organization like Local 183 and I tried
unsuccessfully to persuade him not to run.

There was another Portuguese whom I had hired with an eye
to grooming for the job, Antonio "Tony" Dionisio. Tony was a
bright young man with some Canadian education. He was working as a welder in subway construction when I hired him to be
our first complaints department officer. The complaints department was created because we had so many issues from members
about job sites and there were not enough people in the office

to meet with them and track down the complaints when they came to the office. Of course, it was our job to listen to them but our union representatives were usually out of the office on the job sites or organizing new members. They left the office staff to deal with the guys walking in with complaints. We needed a more efficient way to manage them. Tony's main function was to detail the complaints and channel them to the right union representatives to be dealt with in a speedy manner. In this position, Dionisio developed a fairly good idea of the complexity of the local, which had been my plan for his training. Tony was later promoted to a full-time representative and later to an assistant manager.

Lucas stood a good chance of being elected since at that time a majority of members were Portuguese, hard-working folks who tended to be loyal to each other, pretty much like the Italians. I decided to run which meant I would hold an office at both Local 183 and the district council. I spoke to Reilly, who was like a brother to me, and offered him the positions of secretary treasurer and senior assistant manager. I explained why we had to do this. At first he was resentful but later he came around. A slate was prepared for the nominations supported by all full-time representatives. The candidates on the slate were all elected and I was elected by acclamation. Thus, I found myself running the largest local and the largest district council of the International Labourers Union.

I had recommended that the salary of the local manager, which must be established before nominations, be set at one dollar a year if the position was occupied by a member receiving a full-time salary by another body of the International. To cover both offices I had to rotate from my office at the district council to those of Local 183, dealing with different secretaries and staff and a number of lawyers. It was not easy but I think I managed well and I was always re-elected by acclamation to both positions.

Of course, there were others who saw things differently. Gargaro, for example, found an opportunity to attack me. When I became manager at both the local and the district council, he found a clause in the constitution stating that one person could not hold two full-time positions, although this had been done in the past with Henry Mancinelli. He wrote to the International in Washington asking for me to be removed from one of the offices. At that time, the general president was Angelo Fosco, a good person who always tried to accommodate the locals. He rarely used an iron fist although he had it within his power. He granted me special dispensation, as was his right under the constitution, with one caveat: that I renew the request for special dispensation at each future nomination. I suspect both Coia and Connerton had supported my position with Fosco. Gargaro was eventually defeated at his own local election and Local 506's new manager became Carmine Principato who immediately re-established a relationship of mutual co-operation and respect with the district council, Local 183, and with me personally. From that point, I had no more opposition within the district council other than friendly and sometimes strong differences of opinions with some of the managers of various locals which is only natural in any democratic organization.

While this internal political game was playing out, we started organizing carpenters working in the GTA housing sector, better known as "house framers" and sometimes as "nail bangers." House framers are a special group of building tradesmen. Most of them are paid as pieceworkers, meaning they are paid by the work performed rather than by an hourly rate. Their work is sub-contracted from a main carpenter contractor who, initially, gets his contract from the house builder. House framers are a highly productive group of workers because, obviously, the more they produce the more they earn. They are also a fairly independent bunch of guys. To some of them, hunting and fishing are more important than making money.

To be more precise, the framers' remuneration is based on square footage and the type of house being built, such as single, semi-detached, or townhouse. There are many other factors to take into account when setting the amount they'll be paid, such as how many corners are in the house, the roof's pitch, and whether the garage is separate or incorporated into the house. They usually work in a team of two with some helpers and in effect are really running small businesses. In the GTA at that time, there were around 1,500 framers and we were competing to recruit them against the Carpenters whose local was under the leadership of Gus Simone.

My old friend Gus was an astute operator who merged his Wood, Wire and Metal Lathers International Union with the Carpenters Union and was granted a new charter for the drywallers he came to represent. He saw the end of the plastering industry and of his own trade, "the lather installers." Charlie Irvine, the famous International vice-president of the Operative Plasterers and Cement Mason International Association, fought tooth and nail to block drywall as a new industry in the middle of the 1960s and refused to organize it. Gus chose to embrace it and his local became a strength to be reckoned with in Toronto.

We followed our method of organizing, the slow method of certification, as prescribed by the Labour Relations Act. Gus used the old Irvine method: mass meetings and direct contact with the employers. Arthur Coia tried to make peace between us and held a meeting at the Constellation Hotel up by the airport in Toronto. Given the nature of the industry, it was difficult to make any compromise because the only practical solution was for one side to concede to the other. At the meeting I presented a proposal to Gus which on the surface looked to be a very reasonable compromise but in substance was quite different. Only those familiar with house framing would have sussed out what I was trying to do but Coia and most other building trades' union representatives who worked in the ICI sector thought it was fair. I was playing to Gus's personality: good heart but impetuous.

Gus was upset at my proposal: "No way!" But he did not propose an alternative and missed pointing out the weakness of my "most reasonable proposal."

"You see, Arthur," I said as I left. "I tried but you cannot reason with Gus."

In the spring of 1983 Gus called a carpenters' strike in the manner of Irvine and Zanini. He sent flying squads to a large number of subdivision projects and had a reasonable amount of success. It was a deliberate attempt to expand his union. Many of our members were stopped by intimidation and we were forced to take legal action at the Ontario Labour Relations Board to allow our members to work. The fight was not with the employers: it was about which union had the right to sign which trades and there were more than 2,000 memberships up for grabs. The builders were caught in the crossfire.

It was a time-consuming process before the Labour Board. In many subdivisions, house framing contracts were given to contractors who held agreements with our local, with Gus's local, and also with non-union contractors. We had to use blueprints to map out where Gus was allowed to picket and where he was not. Mike Reilly did a good job on our behalf in limiting Gus's ability to picket. On the other hand, Gus was helped in his cause by a number of key contractors who simply wanted to bring stability to what was becoming a free-for-all.

Gus's strike was reported on the front pages of the Toronto newspapers, particularly because there were a number of "accidental fires." New houses were going up in smoke. Imagine that. Projects in Scarborough and Markham were hit. Four houses were demolished and two were damaged, according to the *Toronto Star*.

While Gus had some important builders on his side, generally the house builders did not like dealing with Gus. They much preferred Local 183's peace-and-stability approach which they had become accustomed to over the years. The same feeling was shared by some main carpenter contractors but after a few weeks of Gus's strike tactics they were ready to capitulate as the "accidental fires" kept happening. I got a call from Tim Armstrong, the Ontario Deputy Minister of Labour, a highly regarded and respected civil servant, to meet with him and John Caruthers, the international vice-president of the Carpenters Union in Canada. Armstrong advised me that the meeting was going to be held on a Saturday in a suite at the Royal York Hotel but that I should to be ready to carry on into Sunday if it became necessary. I don't know why he didn't invite Gus Simone but at that point I knew this was to be the showdown. I went to the meeting on that Saturday morning with Armstrong, Armstrong's assistant, Vic Pathe, a very capable mediator well known for settling difficult labour disputes, and John Carruthers of the Carpenters. After the initial niceties which precede such meetings, Armstrong put down his coffee and leaned in to the table with a serious look on his face. He underlined to all present that the labour dispute was dominating the news media and it was in the public interest to put an end to it. The Ontario government was very concerned, he said, and it was appealing to both sides to use our common sense and play fair and find a satisfactory compromise to end the dispute. He said he admired and respected both of us but that it had to end.

A deep silence followed his appeal and then I said: "We too have the utmost respect for both of you but I am afraid the decision is not in our hands [meaning Carruthers and myself]. It really falls to the Ontario government."

"I don't understand," Armstrong replied.

"Next Tuesday morning there is a meeting between the Premier, the Attorney General, and the Minister of Housing," I said.

Now, Armstrong was surprised that we knew this sensitive information. He nevertheless confirmed the meeting was planned. At that time, we had a good relationship with Pat Kinsella, president of the Ontario Progressive Conservative Party. Earlier, we had made discreet inquiries with Kinsella about some projects being considered which would provide good employment opportunities to our members. He told us the matter was going to be discussed at that meeting.

"Do you mind, Tim, if I speak to my 'brother' John alone?" I asked Tim Armstrong.

"No, go ahead," Tim replied.

So Carruthers and I went into the bedroom of the suite.

"John," I asked. "Do you know why the Premier, the Attorney General, and the Minister of Housing are meeting?"

"No," he replied.

"They are going to call for another Royal Commission inquiry. They are tired of all the sabotage reported in the newspapers. Have you ever been through a Royal Commission?"

"No," replied Caruthers again.

"I have, John," I said, referring to the Waisberg Commission. "I know you are a very honest and good person but can you say the same for certain persons in your union? The commission will check everything, even the bank accounts of your secretary, and if they do not find something, they will look deeper and deeper until eventually they find some skeletons in a closet somewhere. The only way to avoid it is to call off your strike."

John went quiet. He knew a Royal Commission is a serious thing. It's like a Senate or Congressional committee in the U.S. and has far-reaching powers to compel people to testify and to hold them accountable.

We went back to the sitting room of the suite. I saluted my host by saying, "There is nothing really we can discuss, we better wait until after Tuesday," and I left. Both Armstrong and Pathe were none too happy with my play. They had cleared their calendars and obviously were under firm instructions to end the strike and the conflict between the two unions by Sunday.

Gus was holding regular meeting with the strikers every Monday night so at that meeting Gus called off the strike on

Carruthers's direction. It was a failure in the end, although he had come very close to success without knowing it. Despite this, and the ongoing tensions between our unions, we remained friends, which is the way it should be.

Subsequently, Local 183 sped up our organizing efforts. In a short time, we represented 90 per cent of the house framers, adding another 1,500 members to Local 183 taking us to around 10,000 members.

CHAPTER 26

THE GUARDIAN ANGELS

By the middle of the 1980s, interest rates were high again and the Canadian economy was back in recession. Both of those factors had a major impact on the construction industry, raising the costs of mortgages and discouraging people from buying homes. Housing starts, a leading economic indicator, slowed and then plummeted and jobs disappeared. For the union, the recession meant that many of our members were out of work and hungry for jobs. Contractors were hungry, too, and many accepted contracts below cost just to keep their cash flow going, hoping things would turn around soon. The first to pay for this cutthroat competition were our members in the residential sector, and in particular those employed by high-rise forming contractors. These contractors would make their men work before the agreed starting time and after the agreed quitting time without paying for the extra hours. Coffee breaks were outlawed and the men were told to "drink your coffee while you work." Overtime was paid by reducing the hours worked, which meant no overtime pay. Traveling allowances stipulated by the collective agreement were ignored. The contractors even started to cut corners on proper safety procedures.

Under our collective agreement, we had the right to check the concrete forming payroll records, which we did. Everything we checked looked good and this was a problem because word was getting out about the abuses. It did not take long before a small group of forming contractors, headed by Vito Bianchini, a fair and reasonable employer, invited me for coffee to talk about the issue.

"Look," they said, "we are the few that are living up to the agreement, but unless you correct this deteriorating situation quickly we will be forced to follow the bad apples if we want to stay in business."

I told them that we were checking the payroll records and they laughed at me: "Anybody can cook the books."

I had to do something fast. The spectre of the Brandon Hall Group was drifting in front of me. I remembered all too clearly what had happened to them when they failed to come up with a solution to a similar situation. This is why history and life experience are so important. We have to learn the lessons of the past.

I gathered our representatives assigned to the concrete forming industry and asked them to select our most trusted and experienced members from the stewards' list. The plan was to place a full-time man at each of the thirty or so projects we had going at the time. Next we called a weekend meeting with the selected members and briefed them on the plan. It was simple and by the book or, in our case, by the collective agreement. They were tasked with ensuring that our members were not forced to start work before the specified time and that coffee breaks were respected. They were told to write down the name of each member working on the project and his job classification, the hours worked, the location in the event of an applicable travel expense, and, most of all, to be vigilant about safety.

Each Saturday morning, they were to report to the local office with all the information they had gathered during the week. Our booking staff would enter the data into a computer to figure out the weekly pay for each member in each project. On Wednesday evening, the thirty stewards would come back to our office and collect the payroll records prepared by our staff. Payday was on Thursday and their duty was to check every pay stub of our members and compare it to the amounts we had calculated.

There was no way out for the cheating contractors. They knew this and they were forced to comply with the monetary provisions of the collective agreement. Certainly, some tried to sneak around our monitoring but our stewards were always one step ahead of them. One company even tried to avoid paying traveling expenses by asking their employees to report to the company yard where they would be transported to the job in a company vehicle because the collective agreement did specify traveling pay would not be applied in those circumstances. Our members did not like it because it was inconvenient to go to the company yard and then on to the job site. The company transportation scheme was supposed to start at 7 a.m. Our stewards arrived ahead of time and spotted an old beat-up school bus which was clearly going be the transportation vehicle. The driver assigned was the project superintendent. Our steward was not having any of it: "I hope you are not going to drive this old jalopy on the highway with our members on board. They will arrest you!"

The old school bus was probably not that bad but the question of safety was enough for the superintendent to think twice and not drive it. The company ended up paying travel expenses. Six weeks later, the "good" contractors called me in for another coffee.

"Your guardian angels are doing a good job," they told me, smiling. "Contracts are being given out at a normal price and now we can live up to the collective agreement."

The contractors came up with that name, the guardian angels, and it stuck. It was perfect. Nevertheless, we withdrew our guardian angels two months later because it was an expensive program and it had substantially drained Local 183's finances. It had, however, served its purpose. It stabilized the industry and stamped out exploitation, and we gained a reputation for being a vigilant and aggressive organization.

Again, in this business, reputation is everything. In life and in union organizing, it is important not only to present or project yourself as you wish to be known but also to back up your talk with deeds and actions. In dealing with non-union competition, your reputation really does matter because it goes far beyond who you are and your impact on the construction sector as a whole. Non-union contractors are the number one enemy of construction unions and private sector unions in general. Public sector unions do not have to deal with this problem because they are in a monopoly situation. For us in the private sector, it is an issue.

The percentage of non-union contractors in any sector is greatly influenced by the hourly rate and other conditions a union is able to negotiate in that particular sector. A unionized company must compete to win contracts. If it is up against a non-union competitor that pays lower wages, works longer hours, provides shabby working conditions and less safety, and hires and fires at will, the unionized contractor is unlikely to get the job, even though union contractors have better workers and higher productivity. There are two ways for a union to improve its competitiveness: moderate the rates and conditions of unionized employers, which the Brandon Hall leaders failed to do and which was a primary cause of their downfall; or organize the non-union employers. The latter was my primary motive for adopting a strong organizing program.

* * *

Even with me working in two full-time positions, organizing was always at the top of my priority list. At the provincial level, I did it by hiring regional organizers and in Local 183 I organized through our representatives and sometimes by my own efforts. One sector I took a personal interest in was road building, our Achilles heel. We represented about 60 percent of the industry but unfortunately this was reflected in a lower hourly rate. Gazzola Paving was one of the major non-union companies operating in this sector and it was a well-run and respected company. We, together with the Operating Engineers Local 793, tried many times to organize it and failed each time.

The challenge was that the company treated its employees fairly well and paid close to the union rate, although they did not provide the same benefits. Also, many of its employees had been with the company for a number of years and they were loyal to their employer. One day I had the bright idea to call one of the owners, Mark Gazzola, whom I had met once on a picket line years before: "Mark, why don't you sign an agreement with us?"

It was a simple question and Mark was polite and civilized in his response.

"I would if my employees wanted to join your union," Mark replied. To his credit, many non-union employers used more profane language when they spoke to us. We were the enemy in their eyes.

"You know that they would but they are afraid of losing their jobs," I answered back.

Mark laughed and said: "I tell you what, you come to speak to them and, if they agree, I will sign."

"Fine," I said, surprised. Mark had made me an offer I could not refuse. Could it really be that easy?

We arranged a meeting with the employees a couple of days later at 6 a.m. in the company yard. I knew I had to keep it short because they were going off to work so I stood up and quickly summarized the advantages of joining the union. I knew the ace in our hand was our pension benefits so I spent what time I had detailing those. I knew most of them had many years of service with the company and our message would resonate with them.

"Do you know," I explained, "that for every year of service with Gazzola Paving you will be credited with an equal amount of years of contribution to our union pension plan?"

Then I detailed the specific benefits using ten years of service and twenty years of service as examples. Suddenly they became a lot more interested and so I popped the big question: "How many of you wish to join our union? Those in favour, please raise your hand!"

At first there were just a few hands raised but soon those initial hands encouraged others to follow and almost every hand was up. Mark was a man of his word. He signed the agreement and became one of the better union employers. The Operating Engineers Local 793 also benefited from this action since Gazzola signed with them, too. Where our organizers had failed for many years, I was successful with that one call to the right person.

I was not always so lucky. We had other big battles with major non-union contractors including J. K. Beamish and Miller Paving, two of the most established and oldest paving contractors in Ontario. All our organizing effort over the years went for nothing and I had personally tried to organize them without success. Miller Paving and Local 183 had a long history of confrontation. In 1964, Gallagher lobbied the City of Toronto to extend the union clause that applied to its building work to cover all municipal work. The city requires that contractors awarded building contracts from the city be unionized. It made sense to Gallagher that this requirement be extended to city roads, sidewalks, and sewer and water-main projects.

To this end, he and I attended a Metro Toronto controllers meeting one evening at the old City Hall. It lasted until 2 a.m. This was long before amalgamation and back then there were two tiers of local government. Metro was responsible for transit, some parks, water, sewer, major roads, ambulance service, and social services, among other things. The cities, including Toronto, East York, Scarborough, Etobicoke, York, and North York, ran the side streets and smaller city parks, among other things. Aldermen were elected to each city council while controllers were elected at each city or borough level to represent their constituents at the metro level along with the mayor of each partner municipality. Gallagher did a good lobbying job and his request was approved.

However, Miller went to court and in *City of Toronto v. Miller Paving Ltd.* the company was represented by Canadian legal legend J. J. Robinette, who drove home his argument that the extension of the so-called Workmen's Rights Clause in city contracts was outside the city's jurisdiction. The clause was tossed out. The city appealed and again lost. "The by-law is also discriminatory in that it limits the right to tender to those contractors who have contractual relations with only those unions affiliated with the Building Council," the panel of judges wrote. "For that reason it would, in any event, be discriminatory. We would quash the resolution and that part of the bylaw which purports to legislate with respect to the resolution." The city again appealed but two months later, in February 1965, the Supreme Court of Canada refused to hear their arguments.

It reinforced my view that there are no short cuts to organizing. In the 1980s, there were many parking lots being constructed for shopping centres, apartment buildings, and schools. The builders or general contractors required union paving companies. To get around this, both Beamish and Miller formed new companies. These new companies joined the Road Builders Association, giving them a licence to work in union projects while the main companies did non-union work, which was the majority of their revenue. They were having their cake and eating it too, and I came up with a strategy to put an end to it.

At the renewal of our collective agreements (at a different time for each company) we presented the new Beamish and Miller companies with a set of proposals vastly different from those received by other employers. I wanted to get them to refuse to sign which would secure for us the legal right to strike and keep the companies off union projects. The real intention, however, was to organize the parent companies. I had to be careful in negotiations because the law does not allow anyone to expand his bargaining rights through a strike. One can ask for expansion but not strike over it.

Before long, the parent companies grew tired of trading barbs with us over their collective agreements and agreed to a memorandum of understanding, committing themselves to use their union companies for all work performed in the geographical area of the agreement. That was good enough for us. As the old saying goes, there is more than one way to skin a cat.

We also leveraged the law to organize Crupi & Sons, a good road building company which had grown to a respectable size over the years. Again, our organizers had failed to recruit a sufficient number of employees to be certified. One day toward the end of the 1980s, in the middle of the winter, I got a phone call from an old Sicilian member of Local 183 who was a foreman for Malvern Construction, a British company that had operated in Ontario for years. I had personally organized this company in my earlier days and established an almost personal relationship with some of the employees who were very loyal union members.

He told me the weekly cheque paid to them was no longer coming from Malvern Construction but from Crupi & Sons. I immediately investigated and found Crupi had bought out Malvern to expand its road building operation to include sewer and water mains, fields in which different types of machinery and manpower skills are required. We immediately applied for certification for Crupi & Sons since Malvern labourers were our members. The timing of the application was key to our ultimate success. At that moment, road construction was out of season. As a result, the balance of the company's employees was working on sewers and water-mains projects, not on road construction. We were easily able to get the percentage required for certification. The company put up opposition to our request claiming that those employees were merely a fraction of their annual workforce and that their road building operation would commence in the spring. On the surface, it appeared a reasonable argument but the law is clear. It matters only how many employees are signed as a percentage of the total workforce on the day of the application for certification. This was a point in the Ontario Labour Relations Act which was inserted to put an end to the many games contractors had played in the past. With these additional four companies, our percentage of unionized contractors in the road building industry increased substantially. The Operating Engineers Local 793 also benefited from our efforts.

I will close this chapter with a last example of fortune smiling on our organizing efforts. One day, I was in Fred De Gasperis's office to discuss some disputes with companies that he operated when one of his partners entered. Clearly, this person did not know me. He said, "Freddy, the union wants to organize our company. We received notice from the Ministry of Labour." He was refer-ring to our efforts to organize Greenpark Homes, one of the many construction companies with which De Gasperis was associated.

"And what is the problem?" asked De Gasperis with a smile.

"We have given all the work to non-unionized companies."

"Fine," said De Gasperis, turning to me, "we will ask the trade union not to include the projects underway. Strangely enough, we have just the right person here. John, do you agree?"

I did not know if our organizers had actually made that request to the OLRB for certification, so I said: "Let me make a phone call first."

I called my assistant manager, Lou Castaldo, who told me we had indeed made an application but still did not have suf-ficient members to get certification. This was standard operating procedure. If we ended up at a standstill in recruiting, our prac-tice was to apply for certification in the hope that the posting of the notice by the employer at the place of employment, as required by the Labour Act, would encourage others to sign up.

From that point, workers have a week to decide whether to sign or oppose certification. In the majority of cases, the employer will use the interval to lean on the workers to oppose certification. I explained De Gasperis's proposal to Castaldo who quickly said I should take it because it was probably our only hope. Returning to De Gasperis, I said: "Freddy, it is very important to have good relations between us, so we accept your proposal."

De Gasperis turned to the man who had come in to us and said, "See, I told you there was no problem!"

Carlo Baldassara later took control of Greenpark and transformed it into the biggest luxury home building company in Canada, creating thousands of jobs. He is another example of a non-English-speaking, poorly educated immigrant with a sharp mind who made a major contribution to the prosperity of Canada. Like so many others, he would not be allowed in under Trudeau's point system.

These were just a few of the methods and strategies we used to expand Local 183. It is much like a bricklayer laying one brick on top of another. We also built our union by signing up workers and companies, one by one, doing it the right way, the legal way. It was hard work to become the biggest construction local in Canada and the only one fully organized in the residential sector in North America but the benefits to the members speak for themselves.

Our organizing abilities were recognized by our International. For example, in the 1980s I was asked by vice-president and regional manager Max Warren to speak to delegates of his California region at a conference in Honolulu about organizing. Of course I accepted, and I was looking forward to spending a few days at Waikiki Beach. The only downside was that Max had to move the delegates' meeting from Waikiki to the other side of the island because the hotel workers were on strike and we ended up at Turtle Bay, which was lovely but it is a surfer's beach with ten-foot waves. No place for a quiet afternoon on the sand.

CHAPTER 27

THE BOMBSHELL AGREEMENT

By 1987, the Canadian economy had improved and a combination of lower interest rates and a new and more generous capital gains tax regime, introduced by Brian Mulroney's government, created a boom in the residential construction industry. I was always proud to represent the most productive workers in North America and, for that matter, in the world, and so with the reinvigorated economy and housing starts rising, I thought it was time to reward our members with some good increases in wages and benefits because we had been running tight during the recession.

Our residential construction collective agreements were expiring at the end of April that year. I had many off-the-record conversations with key employers in each industry, testing the waters at breakfasts, lunches, or simply over a cup of coffee. In addition to gathering intelligence, I was also spreading my gospel: "It is time to compensate productive workers with a good increase."

Most of those employers I met with individually agreed with me. I took the matter further and explored a range of increases

I thought would be appropriate as these casual discussions continued. The only obstacle was that none of the six employer associations in the residential sector wanted to be the first to sign, setting the pattern for the others. So I came up with an idea: no one goes first. We do all of them at the same time.

Much easier said than done. Each association had different problems, different personalities, and different lawyers. The same was true on our side with our six committees but I decided to give it a go anyway. Meetings were arranged with all of the employers on the same day, at the same time and place. We met at the Skyline Hotel on Dixon Road in Toronto in twelve different meeting rooms, one for each committee on either side of the six negotiations. I assigned a senior representative to each union committee with Reilly assigned to the house framing committee because I considered it the most complicated, even though I had already done a lot of spadework with key house framing contractors. We had agreed to a framework settlement and I briefed Reilly on the details.

I took a suite in the hotel and with me was Al Minsky, our lawyer. I had learned from bitter experience that it was important to write down, precisely, the terms of settlement. Increases are easy to remember but the language of a deal is always subject to interpretation unless clearly recorded, preferably by a lawyer. I did not have the luxury of stopping to write down the terms of every settlement because I had to move from room to room and keep the action going. My instruction to our committees was to advise me if they hit a major stumbling block at which point I could intervene personally. My big concern was that one of the six associations would bolt, creating a domino effect, so it was crucial to keep everyone talking constantly.

During the day nothing was agreed upon but there were some frank exchanges of opinion. We all enjoyed a good dinner that night and the atmosphere became more relaxed. At about 2 a.m. I went for broke and started in with the high-rise forming association and reached a deal with the contractors. One down, five to go.

I left our lawyer to write down the terms of settlement, instructing him to join me at my next stop, the house basement contractors. Bang. Another settlement was reached. I kept going, next to concrete and drain, and then to the high-rise apartment builders and on to the low-rise builders. By 8 a.m. we had signed memoranda of settlement with five employers' associations. I was relieved—and exhausted.

There was one more contract to finish. I went to the house framing meeting room expecting that there would be a memorandum already finalized. After all, I had already done the heavy lifting with key contractors. Much to my surprise, I found the employers getting ready to leave, upset over the lack of progress and talking about some major differences which had arisen during the night. They were all exhausted and it was a bit of a problem to convince them to stay but I managed it and went into our committee's room to be briefed on why this deal had gone off the rails. I took charge and picked up the pieces to keep the negotiations going, keeping the two sides apart to prevent a flare-up. I literally went back and forth from our committee room to the employers, exploring compromises. By 2 p.m., the time was ripe to bring them together and a tentative settlement was reached. We shook hands, with both sides relieved by the outcome and agreeing to recommend the deal to their constituents for ratification.

We were just about to leave when John Deverell, the *Toronto Star* labour reporter, dropped in to see how things were going. He grabbed a few quotes and took a picture of our house framing negotiating committee because they were the only ones still hanging around. *The Star* published a story with his byline, headlined: "The man behind bombshell pay hikes—Labour chief sets building industry precedent."

This time, the headline was bang-on. It was truly a bombshell settlement. The increases ranged between $3 and $5 an hour, which at the time was good money. Deverell's story ran in the Sunday *Star*:

John Stefanini, architect of a bombshell $3-plus hourly wage increase for 7,000 Metro construction workers, has finally revealed the union power he's been creating for more than two decades.

The business manager of Laborers Local 183 on Wednesday summoned six groups of home and apartment building contractors to the Skyline Hotel for what some chose to call negotiations. It was the unveiling of Stefanini's plans for the housing industry.

Within 11 hours, five contractor groups had acquiesced to big wage hikes for their Metro-area employees—a precedent which within a year may shatter the entire system of construction industry bargaining in Ontario.

After a further 19 hours of haggling over piecework rates, the house-framing carpentry contractors signed. This completed the union chief's design for two years of stability in Metro's overheated residential construction sector.

"It's like going fishing," chortled the shirt-sleeved, cigar-smoking Stefanini on Thursday morning as he manoeuvred the last group into the union's net. "Once you've got the hook in, you have to keep tension on the line."

Deverell went on to describe the thirty hours without sleep and how I went from room to room and he also noted how far we had come:

With last week's spectacular wage increases Stefanini has reached a long-sought plateau. For the first time his residential high-rise concrete forming members will get higher pay than the labourers, carpenters, ironworkers and masons doing concrete work on projects like the Dome Stadium. Previously these industrial-commercial sector agreements have always led construction wage setting.

"They've always looked down on us, but those days are over,"
says Stefanini, delighted that his residential sector is now well
organized enough to shed its lower-wage tradition.

Deverell also described how I managed to shake up the construction union scene and I have to say he was more than
complimentary in his detailing of the evolution of Local 183 and
my leadership role in raising the bar for the entire construction
industry:

Stefanini smiles as he contemplates the conundrum he has created
for the others. Then—by describing his own union—he outlines his
vision for revolutionizing construction unionism.

"Our road to higher wages has been through higher productiv-
ity," he says. "We have built this union outside every concept of
building trades unionism that came before. Instead of fighting new
technology—in concrete forming, in tunneling, in pouring base-
ments, in prefab housing—we accept it and adapt to it."

Under Stefanini, Laborers 183, scorned by others as the lowest
of the 'mud trades,' has responded by showing little respect for the
craft jurisdiction of the other construction unions.

In another daring heresy, Laborers 183 has almost completely
abolished the hiring hall, the key institution of craft unions.

Local 183 employers choose their own workers subject only to
the requirement that they pay union wages and benefits. The elimi-
nation of union job dispatching allows workers to stay together and
move from one job to the next as production teams.

The endless jurisdictional disputes between carpenters, labour-
ers, masons, and ironworkers vanish when all are members of the
same union. Local 183 collect 25 cents per hour in union dues, and
maintains 25 business agents to enforce its contracts.

In recent years Local 183 has been spreading its multi-craft
organization into the industrial-commercial-institutional sector, to
the dismay and horror of the traditional craft unions.

To the accusation that he is a wage-cutter with a sweetheart philosophy, Stefanini waves his $3-an-hour settlement and replies that construction unions are mistaken to swim against the tide of technology.

Devoting the main energy of union business agents to the preservation of traditional craft boundaries is a sterile exercise, he suggests, and ultimately damaging to all construction unionism.

Instead Laborers Local 183 has been concentrating on providing benefits and services to members—grievance procedure, skills training, a pension plan, health insurance, a dental clinic, and a credit union.

Looking back on that story, I find myself nodding in agreement with my own words. They were prophetic but they also reflected my philosophy since the beginning. Time does not stand still and neither does technology or the techniques used in the construction industry. For example, drywall replaced plastering but the tradesmen shifted to become drywallers and mudders and carried on working, as they should.

Flying concrete forms became the standard in high-rise construction and we provided a single labour solution instead of having to organize crews with three or four different trade unions.

Our labourers may have been scorned as the "mud" trades at one time, those digging ditches and carrying materials, but little by little we organized them into a skilled workforce. Our union provided training to build their skills and make them an integral part of a construction project. Together with essentials like health care, a pension plan, a dental clinic and a credit union, Local 183 had truly grown to become a beneficial force to be reckoned with, always on the side of the members and striving to raise them up year after year, contract after contract.

CHAPTER 28

CHANGING OF THE GUARD

Pierre Trudeau's drastic changes to immigration laws not only put a stop to Italians coming in numbers to Canada but Europeans from non-English- and non-French-speaking countries were also shut out. He opened the doors wide to refugees, however, so much so that hundreds of thousands rushed to our shores. Our incredibly generous, taxpayer-funded social-security benefits made Canada all the more attractive. These benefits included free dental care and prescription drugs, things to which many working Canadians were not entitled. It was also easy to claim refugee status.

This had a major impact on Local 183. Thousands of Portuguese landed at Pearson International Airport and with the advice of unscrupulous immigration consultants claimed refugee status on the grounds that they were persecuted at home for being Jehovah's Witnesses, never mind that some were wearing gold crucifixes that identified them as Roman Catholics. Nonetheless, the Portuguese had not come to take advantage of our generous benefits. They wanted to work. Generally, I have found the

Portuguese to be a hard-working people and I thank God they came to Canada with other non-English-speaking nationalities to contribute to our economy.

The fact is that without illegal immigrants like these the residential construction industry would have suffered a serious shortage of workers that would have substantially increased the cost of homes. Of course, I am opposed to illegal immigration in principle. I waited for more than two years in Rome before being granted an immigration visa and I followed the rules. However, the present immigration system, designed to protect the French language, is based on points, with two of the most important criteria being education and knowledge of our official languages. The system accepts educated immigrants who come to the country wanting good jobs. This creates more competition for young Canadian university graduates, our sons and daughters whom we have educated at considerable expense. It also assumes that our sons and daughters will perform the so-called humble and heavy jobs, chopping wood and fetching water, since the immigration policy does not bring in this kind of worker. Many employers cannot find the skilled or semi-skilled workers they require. The upshot is that provinces like Ontario are experiencing a shortage of the kind of workers that were the backbone of our economy until Trudeau's changes. He introduced a bad policy.

While they did not speak one of the official languages and had limited education, the entrepreneurial spirit and work ethic of these earlier generations of immigrants served us well. Many went on to launch businesses of incredible scale such as Magna International, Royal Plastic, and Saputo Cheese, to mention just a few among many thousands of entrepreneurial case studies. It is hard to imagine what our economy would look like without these thousands of businesses.

Immigration policies should be based on two pillars: humanitarian aspects, such as family reunification, and the needs of the Canadian economy. Our economy requires all kinds of immigrants, from the highly educated to the skilled, semi-skilled, and unskilled. There are many jobs Canadians will not take, a reality which is true in many industrialized countries.

We should also protect bilingualism. It enriches the nation and we should be proud of our French and English official languages. But we can take it too far. In 2002, federal Minister of Citizenship and Immigration Elinor Caplan introduced even more stringent rules regarding language requirements. In response, David Crane, the former *Toronto Star* economics editor wrote a couple of columns noting that people like Frank Stronach, who built the Magna auto parts empire, would not be admitted under the new rules. "If Canada's new immigration rules, sneakily announced by Immigration Minister Elinor Caplan just before Christmas, had been in effect when a young Stronach had applied to come here, he would not have been allowed into Canada," wrote Crane. "The Austrian-born graduate of his country's apprenticeship system would not have had adequate entry points. Yet Stronach has created thousands of jobs in Canada, as have other immigrants who would not be allowed in Canada today."

Crane said it "is hard to imagine a more short-sighted and reactionary immigration policy than the one Citizenship and Immigration Minister Elinor Caplan snuck through. . . . Her rigid new policy ignores Canada's changing demographics. Immigrants now account for about 70 per cent of Canada's labour force growth and, as Caplan has admitted, will grow to 100 per cent in the not-too-distant future as Canadians continue to age."

I saw all of this coming. In the fall of 1986, I was invited to meet with the Portuguese Authority in Lisbon. Along with two of our Portuguese representatives, Tony Lucas and Tony Dionisio, I brought along Joe Carraro, also a fluent Portuguese speaker, and Carmine Principato, the business manager of Labourers Local 506. I also reached out to the Canadian Labour Congress. They sent Secretary Treasurer Richard Mercier to join our group and add some prestige since we were going to meet the president and prime minister of Portugal.

In Lisbon we were well received by President Mario Soares and Prime Minister Cavaco Silva. We were also warmly greeted by Ms. Manuela Aguirar, a very attractive and gracious woman, who held the title of Secretary of the Community, the equivalent of a minister in our government.

On a personal note, I took advantage of the trip to visit the Fatima Basilica complex. I also went to Lucas's village in the north of Portugal and Dionisio's hometown, close to the sea. I came away convinced that Canada needs more immigrants like the Portuguese who only want to work hard and build a better country. I strongly disagreed with the former Immigration Minister Jason Kenney who once said we should insist on the knowledge of language to better integrate immigrants. Tell that to the Ukrainians who opened the west and the many other ethnic groups who are now fully integrated into Canadian society but who came to this blessed country without speaking a word of English or French.

This was long before our multiculturalism policies were established. Sadly, some other immigrant groups, while they have a knowledge of the language, are reluctant or find it difficult to integrate into the dominant culture. And again, why should they bother? Is this not a multicultural country?

Toward the end of the 1980s, the federal government was talking about deporting thousands of illegal Portuguese immigrants. I considered it my duty to do something about it because I represented thousands of them through Local 183. I also knew from personal experience what a terrifying thing it is to be threatened with deportation. It had left a bitter taste that I carried for years. I was also concerned about the economy because losing all those workers would cripple the residential construction industry. One of our employers' trustees, Don Andrew, had a good political connection with Barbara MacDougall, the federal minister of immigration. He arranged a meeting with her at a downtown hotel suite. There we pointed out the contribution of the illegal Portuguese immigrants and asked her to legalize their status. MacDougall understood both the humanitarian and economic problems and suggested that if any "illegal immigrants" were to return to Portugal, she would instruct the Canadian Embassy to issue them (excepting those with criminal records) a permanent resident visa they could use to return to Canada.

We shook hands on the deal although she cautioned us to keep everything discreet because other nationalities with thousands of illegal immigrants were also asking for amnesty. To facilitate the resident visas, we opened a special office at the Galleria Shopping Centre at Dupont and Dufferin, staffed with Portuguese-speaking employees. Local 183 contributed $50,000, Local 506 $25,000, and a number of other contractor associations made additional donations. A special letter was given to applicants to be presented to the Canadian embassy in Lisbon. Everything went like clockwork. More than 14,000 Portuguese went home, visited the Canadian embassy there, presented their letters, and were given a visa to return with residency status. Ironically, the majority were not even members of the Laborer's Union. The Portuguese community owes thanks to Barbara MacDougall and the Mulroney Conservatives.

In 1993, after my retirement, the Portuguese government awarded me a gold medal to commemorate my efforts on behalf of those immigrants. I treasure it and it has a special place among other awards, such as the Award of Merit presented to me by Toronto Mayor Art Eggleton on March 9, 1989, and the President's Award from the prestigious National Italian American Foundation, which was facilitated by LIUNA General Secretary Treasurer Arthur E. Coia.

CHAPTER 29

MY CAREER AS A DEVELOPER

While I was manager of both Local 183 and the provincial District Council, I spent more of my time on the affairs of the Council. This narrative, however, is focused on how Local 183 was built so references to my other activities, such as managing the Council, are not discussed in detail although that experience was a rich one, full of many interesting events and personalities. I enjoyed my time dealing with fourteen managers from across the province and it was a challenge because, like me, most had strong personalities and were intelligent, motivated, dedicated labour leaders.

Every time I met with them in their cities I was well received and taken to the best restaurants. Sometimes I went fishing and hunting with them. This does not mean there were no controversies. Occasionally, there were major differences on policies and programs and at times it got heated but it never descended to a personal level. Each of us was doing his best for his members.

While the District Council constitution did grant me some special powers, I tried to refrain from using them because I wanted to ensure a good balance between the Council and the Locals. I certainly did not want to make the Council stronger at the Locals' expense. I felt that by making the Locals stronger, the Council would ultimately benefit.

Ontario, again, is a big territory and within the province there are substantial regional differences. The Greater Toronto Area is densely populated, urban with a lot of commercial and residential construction. The far north is cold and harsh and construction is driven by resource development. To the southwest, you have a mix of agriculture around London and auto manufacturing around Windsor and petrochemicals around Sarnia. All these areas present their Locals with unique needs and wants.

As I have mentioned, the Council provision of our constitution was written, in my opinion, for a more limited geographical area such as New York or Chicago where there are numerous Locals chartered by the International Union. Ontario being different, my policy was to emphasize progress over control. During province-wide negotiations, the real bargaining took place among our fourteen managers. Each, for good reasons, thought that his area was most important. The managers were united, however, in their dislike for Toronto. This is not unusual since not only does the rest of Ontario dislike Toronto, the rest of Canada dislikes Toronto. The city is too rich, too big, too loud, too aggressive, too money-oriented, and too self-absorbed, according to those who do not live there. Those of us who live in Toronto, of course, are puzzled at this reaction. We see Toronto as the best city in the world. Why would anyone want to live anywhere else? The same dynamics probably exist around the national or state capitols in most countries.

All of this is important background to a set of negotiations that triggered the inclusion of the Construction Management Clause into collective agreements used by a number of Ontario construction unions.

During the 1980s, a new phenomenon took place in construction industry. General contractors had long been bound by their collective agreements to sublet work only to other union-ized companies. The owners of large construction projects found a way around this requirement by hiring general contractors not as general contractors but as consultants or construction manag-ers. The owners, in these instances, would retain the authority to sublet contracts for each trade to whoever they choose, including non-union contractors. In the beginning this practice was iso-lated but by the middle of the 1980s, it became more prevalent.

If we had let this go unchallenged, it would have weak-ened construction trade unions. In fact, it had already impacted Alberta's construction unions where the practice was widespread. Accordingly, all of the Ontario construction unions were up in arms, particularly the so-called mud-trades, which were the most affected.

In 1988, it became a strike issue. An ICI multi-trades, prov-ince-wide strike would not have been an ordinary strike. At that time, there were over 25,000 workers employed in this sector and their walking off the job would have hurt the provincial econ-omy, if not the Canadian economy. That was a steep price to pay but we were determined to kill the new practice before it could do further damage to our workers. The general contractors said they were sympathetic to us but their hands were tied. They had to comply with the way owners were structuring their contracts.

In April, we attended a Toronto meeting of all mud trades at the downtown Holiday Inn. It was organized by Joe Kennedy, manager of Operating Engineers Local 793. Joe was a man who dared to walk where angels feared to tread. While he claimed to be left-wing in his politics, he often associated with conservative politicians, saying that he was a fiscal conservative although his heart was with the left. In a departure from the standard position of many union leaders, he saw employers as "partners." To most in the union movement, that was a radical position but Joe's philosophy was that if they prosper, we prosper. He nevertheless defended the interests of his members and the work jurisdiction of his union.

Joe and I were sometimes good friends and other times bitter enemies. Most of the conflict between us was over the operation of small pieces of equipment such as Bobcats, which I called Tonka Toys. These were small diggers and shearing machines operated by a single person. They required limited training or skill, nothing like the big cranes and other giant machines run by the Operating Engineers. Joe believed Bobcat operators belonged in the Operating Engineers. I did not agree. All unions have conflicts with other unions from time to time over things like this, each claiming jurisdiction.

At the meeting Joe proposed two things: first, no union would deal with any other issue on the table until the question of construction management was resolved and, second, that we appoint one person to represent all six unions to negotiate with whoever was appointed by the Ontario General Contractors Association as its negotiator. It did not take much for all six unions to agree. Joe then caught me by surprise when he put my name forward as the representative of the six unions. I was even more shocked when the other unions agreed. There were some bitter rivalries over work jurisdiction among our unions. I wondered if they had confidence in me or if they were hoping I would fail and embarrass myself.

Either way, it was a very difficult issue and I accepted the challenge. My pride left me no choice. The contractors chose Brian Foote, the labour relations director of the Toronto Construction Association as their representative and both of us agreed to be assisted by lawyers because the issue was delicate and required legal input. Our lawyer was Al Minsky and their lawyer was Bruce Benning, both well-known in the labour community.

We met a week later at the Constellation Hotel. Each union had its full negotiating committee in a separate meeting room and the Ontario Contractors Association had its own meeting room. I had a separate room, as did Brian Foote, and each of our lawyers. The game kicked off at 10 a.m. with the usual courtesies exchanged over a cup of coffee. It was not all daggers and swords. Brian had a sense of humour and a loud laugh. All of us were genuinely interested in a solution and we would make good faith efforts to find it.

The contractors' position was simple: if owners hire us as construction consultants, we cannot force them to sublet work only to union contractors. If we refuse to act as construction consultants, there are plenty of others who will, and we will lose lucrative contracts and ultimately the unions will suffer.

We worked and talked all day to find a compromise but failed. From time to time, I made the rounds of various committee rooms to advise them of the progress or, in reality, lack of it. At the end of the day, we adjourned until morning.

By the end of the second day, we still had no agreement and people were frustrated. At about 11 p.m., I went to the labourers' committee room and found them ready to explode. One of my own people launched an attack on me, saying: "What is so difficult in telling the general contractors to just sublet work to union companies?"

It was a perfectly legitimate question but there was no simple answer. We were in new territory and the issues were complex. With the situation getting out of control, I knew I had to nip the frustration in the bud. I let them vent for a bit and then, in an angry and commanding voice, reminded them that general contractors were happy to sublet work only to union companies when they were in control of the situation but when they were acting as consultants or construction managers, the owner held all the cards and we had no agreement with the owner. He could do what he wanted. "We are here to find a solution to this problem," I said, "Is it clear now?"

That calmed them down and, strangely enough, a solution occurred to me as I was driving home that night at 2 a.m.

The next morning, we were back at it for 10 a.m. and I came in to find the others sipping coffee. "I have a solution," I said, rather dramatically, and they all burst out laughing. They thought I was joking. I let them have some fun and then got down to work.

"Up to now, we have discussed and disagreed on what a general contractor should do as a construction management consultant," I said. "Why don't we agree on what they cannot do?"

Now I had their attention. I explained my thinking in detail. Instead of trying to talk the general contractors out of working as consultants and construction managers, we would draft a new clause with greater emphasis on what they could not do in that role. In short, the clause would forbid them from assisting owners in selecting subcontractors unless those subcontractors were unionized. Because the owners were generally incapable of finding subcontractors on their own, this meant, as a practical matter, that a general contractor working as a consultant or construction manager would be asked to recommend subcontractors, and because of existing agreements they would only recommend union shops.

This blocking strategy was simply a new application of the old saying, "if you cannot overcome an obstacle, go around it." It is an approach that has served me well over the years. Each committee fully endorsed the compromise and a province wide ICI strike was averted. All monetary issues were settled by each union with their respective employer since there was already a common understanding of the bottom-line monetary increase. Contractors found a way out of the trap, owners were forced to contract with unions, and we avoided a slow painful death.

* * *

Against all these changes in the way the construction industry operated we were also seeing a lot of changes at the membership level. For one, our office on Dupont Street was crowded by the mid-1980s and the membership was still growing rapidly. We lacked both space and parking so we had to find new headquarters.

At first I thought about the old Dufferin Construction yard on Dufferin Street, south of Lawrence Avenue West. It was fifteen acres in a good location but the starting price for negotiations was just under $2 million. Some executive board members and one in particular thought that was too high.

By coincidence, I was in a phase in which I was telling myself that I should listen more often to other people (although, as I ultimately discovered, it is usually better for a leader to lead than follow). The price for that property more than doubled in a short period of time and I cursed myself for not following my instinct. North York City Councillor Mario Gentile then directed our attention to four houses for sale at the corner of Downsview Avenue and Ridge Road, each with a huge long lot. We took a look and bought them. The problem was that the area was zoned residential and had no connection to a main street. We needed both a rezoning and a strip of land to access Wilson Avenue.

Thanks to our political connections we were able to purchase a strip of land from the Ontario Ministry of Transportation to connect us with Wilson Ave. The price was fairly high because at that time real estate was going crazy but we had no real alternative. Next, we needed rezoning. North York's Mayor Mel Lastman was sympathetic to our rezoning request but insisted we get our new neighbours to approve it. We called a series of evening meetings at the nearby Triumph Hotel and invited local residents. Now I was not only the business manager of two large union organizations, I was also playing the role of a land developer.

Initially, the residents were opposed but when I told them that our other option was to build a non-profit townhouse complex, they quickly changed their minds. We conceded a number of points requested by the residents which were fair and reasonable and once we had their support, rezoning was easy.

I was determined to build a new office complex which would suit the needs of Local 183 for many, many years to come. As I considered all this, I reviewed what we had done in the past. Each time we bought or built a new building we took on what seemed like a huge mortgage, yet we paid it off in a reasonable time. I was not afraid of another large mortgage although I did have other concerns. I wanted the new building to be very large and well designed. In the old building every time it rained there was a bottleneck at the narrow front door, making it hard to get in and out. This time I wanted something more like a shopping centre, with different entrances for different services such as the union office, social services, the dental clinic, and trust fund administration. We also needed a large meeting hall since it was always a problem for us to find a hall. I thought we could connect the two wings of the complex with a hall for both special meetings and regular membership meetings.

The board supported me and we engaged an architect, filled him in on our ideas, and set him to work on the details. I also insisted on a clock tower out front, a monument to fallen construction workers, and, as a special aesthetic touch, archways all around in a reproduction of a typical Northern Italian piazza or town square. These were important details. Our union is not just an organization: it is a symbol of the rights of workers. It represents the strength we find in joining together to speak as one voice, much as a church represents the strength of its congregation. Besides, a town square is always more attractive than another parking lot and I wanted the building to be welcoming to our members and visitors alike. Every piazza needs a central focus and ours was the monument to fallen construction workers. It was very important to me and, I believe, to our members. I engaged two Italian artists, Antonio Selva and Giovanni Fanton, who had done many altars and statues in Toronto churches. I also wanted a figure that truly represented the construction workers and I came up with the concept of a worker with a jackhammer looking down with respect and dignity.

With all this spinning in the background, I still found time to visit Rome and while having breakfast there with Gord Wilson, the president of the Ontario Federation of Labour, I was suddenly inspired. I grabbed a serviette and scribbled down the basics of what would later be inscribed at the base of the monument:

In memory of those who lost their lives to build a better community.

I also wrote a dedication for the clock tower:

We came from many lands
United we stand
In a Union strong and free
In equality and dignity

I have to note that Gord made some useful edits and corrections.

Incidentally, we were in Rome attending a meeting of INAS-CANADA, an organization founded by the Italian trade unions to assist Italian immigrants in Canada to obtain Italian pension benefits. Italy is very generous in extending pension benefits to its emigrants. Any Italian emigrant that has at least one year of making tax contributions in Italy or who performed military service in Italy can have their years of residence in Canada credited as years of contribution to the Italian Government Pension Plan (INPS). At that time, the eligible age for Italian pension benefits was fifty-five for women and sixty for men. The benefits would be recalculated when the Italian emigrant received his or her Canadian pension. By the end of the 1980s, some $250 million per year was being sent by Italy to Italians in Ontario alone, a significant contribution to the Canadian economy.

The problem with Italian pensions, however, was bureaucracy and red tape. Most immigrants found it hard to apply. To assist them, the Italian trade unions established the *patronati* in Canada. These are social assistance organizations, free of charge, for immigrants. The services were paid by the Italian trade unions which in turn got Italian government grants based on the number of immigrants they assisted. Additional help came from INAS-Canada which was jointly administered by Canadian and Italian trade unionists. Local 183 was and is a major support to INAS-CANADA, providing it with rent-free office space. The Ontario government, under Liberal Premier David Peterson, also recognized the importance of the *patronati* and on my request provided a grant of $200,000.

Back in Canada, we were forging ahead with the new head-quarters. We engaged Erskine Developments as the lowest bidder to be our construction consultant. Harold Green was the second lowest and so both of us were disappointed. We insisted that the concrete forming work be performed by our members, although it was an ICI project. The building committee was the executive board of Local 183 and we met with the construction manager early in the morning each week and awarded each contract, as per their recommendation after reviewing bids by invited companies, usually a dozen for each trade.

Costs skyrocketed during the construction period, 1988 to 1990, but we felt our expenses were reasonable considering the complexity of the project. The dental clinic, for instance, had to have a special wall to contain the radiation spillage from X-ray equipment. The total area of the complex was around 130,000 square feet above ground, with underground parking, a commer-cial kitchen for the new hall, a restaurant, and all the features we could tick off from our wish list and still stay within the initial budget. Remember, this was the biggest single union building in all of Canada. Not bad considering that we had a three-room office when I first walked in the door.

In September 1990 we had our official inauguration of the complex. We invited Ontario Premier Bob Rae, his Minister of Labour, Robert MacKenzie, North York Mayor Mel Lastman, our International Union representatives, the Ontario Federation of Labour, and representatives from almost all the major labour movements. It was a wonderful day. We marched from Wilson

Avenue along the newly named Solidarity Boulevard to Union Square (also newly named). The sound of bagpipes from the 48th Highlanders Regiment filled the air and in front of the monument of the fallen construction workers at the square we had several religious ceremonies, first by an Aboriginal shaman, and then by a Rabbi, followed by Catholic and Protestant priests.

After the ribbon cutting, we went into the big hall where there was folk music and dancers from the various cultures, races, and communities represented by Local 183—Aboriginal, Italian, Portuguese, Latin American, and others. Of course, the food also covered all the bases and then, for the big finale, we held the official opening with all those dignitaries and the wail of the 48th Highlanders.

The local executive had approved my suggestion that the new meeting hall be called the Gerry Gallagher Hall. It was a fitting tribute to a man who had played such a pivotal role in getting the labour movement off the ground in Toronto, a man who paved the way for so many. Gerry Gallagher was also one of the first inductees to the Canadian Labour Hall of Fame. Gerry's name had been on the previous training centre, next door to our old Dupont Street offices, and this was an extension of that. We had opened that building in the spring of 1979 and, sadly, Gerry had passed away around Labour Day the year before. I never forgot the man who first hired me and gave me a shot. For that matter, I have never forgotten anyone who worked with us and walked with us from those early days. For all our differences, we are ultimately on the same side.

It was quite an emotional moment for me. Our present is and was and always will be defined by our past. Our past, my past, only served to reinforce my principles and ensure that I would always honour those who were such an integral part of our history. It was the wily Joe Kennedy who drove this realization home for me. He had invited me to a Christmas dinner of the Operating Engineers Local 793 and I found myself and Rita sitting at the main table with the Ontario Minister of Labour and Wesley Lippett, past manager of Operating Engineers Local 793, whom Joe had defeated in the previous election. I knew that there was bad blood between the two so we got on the best we could without getting into anything. A few days later I asked Joe why Wes had been at the main table with us.

"He was our past manager and he deserved to be honoured," replied Joe, adding something I will always remember: "If we forget our past, we have no future."

* * *

Being a union is about more than just negotiating wages and working conditions. One of the big responsibilities is training. Because we had acquired the rights to represent a number of trades in the construction industry, it also became Local 183's responsibility to supply contractors with skilled workers. The construction industry is changing constantly and new skills are part of this evolutionary process. The so-called common labourer, for example, is a thing of the past. A labourer today is a skilled tradesperson. He must know and understand the rules and laws around job safety, the proper use of chemicals, the handling of materials, and many other aspects which contribute to productivity and safety on the job. A concrete forming contractor once told me a good labourer is more important than other tradesmen.

Our first training centre was in an empty factory next to our old offices. It was quite something, because we had some special requirements such as the ceiling height of more than thirty-six feet in order to install a flying form system within the building. Our training methods were hands-on. We recreated the environment and operations of a construction site. After creating the training centre, as each collective agreement was renewed, we also negotiated a contribution to the training fund. The fund was administered jointly with the employers giving each sector in the construction industry the right to appoint a trustee. It was truly a joint labour-and-management enterprise with Harold Green representing the apartment builders. He was quite active and played a constructive role in the development of many training programs. Our first training director was Joe Carraro who founded COSTI and had considerable experience in this area. We hired Eddie Thornton, an Irish carpenter who had a wide practical knowledge of construction as his number two, and together Eddie and Joe did a great job.

Now, as we opened our new building, we were also looking for a new training centre because we had become a victim of our own success and had outgrown our original centre. In 1990, we bought ten acres of land on Huntington Road, just north of Highway 7. There was an historical farmhouse that we decided to retain and incorporate into the training complex. The Training and Rehabilitation Trust Fund engaged an architect and called for bids. This time Harold Green's company was the low bidder. We had the fund's lawyer prepare a form to disclose a potential conflict of interest since Harold was a trustee of the fund, and all the trustees approved Harold's bid and role. There was a full-time construction supervisor on the job but Harold was quite often present and hands-on. I have to say he put his heart into the project, treating it as he would have treated the building of his own home. The new training complex has 30,000-square feet of shops as well as 3,000 square feet of classrooms and administration offices. Just before my retirement, the trustees unanimously adopted a motion to dedicate the new centre with my name.

* * *

Workers injured on the job, and how to avoid injuries, have always been leading concerns for our union. If an injured worker is able to return to work, then the only problem is finding him a job. If an injured worker is totally disabled, then he is entitled to a full Workmen's Compensation Board pension. The most difficult problems occur when an injured worker's disability will not allow him to return to his regular occupation but is not serious enough to qualify him for a full pension. In such cases a doctor's certificate specifies he is fit for "light work." There is no such a thing as "light work" in the construction industry. The injured worker needs to be retrained to perform some other kind of work that falls under the "light work" definition.

When planning the layout of the new building we assigned space for retraining workshops. Since we also represented building maintenance employees, we thought injured construction workers would be suitable for this type of work, which is much less physical than construction. Through our Training and Rehabilitation Trust Fund, we hired specialized instructors and installed the necessary equipment to teach maintenance basics: how to repair tiles, adjust doors, paint, clean, and do some basic plumbing and electrical work. The Workmen's Compensation Board, as it was known then, contributed financially on a per diem, per capita basis.

Unfortunately, not everything on my wish list came to fruition in rehabilitation programs for injured workers. I had long been interested in occupational health issues since they affected so many of our members. Back in 1982, Charles Caccia, the federal Minister of Labour, appointed me to the Canadian Occupational Health and Safety Board of Governors. This board, headquartered in Hamilton, met monthly in various cities across Canada and comprised labour management professionals such as doctors and federal bureaucrats. The most controversial issues dealt with by the board concerned occupational health and I got a front-row seat and an education. Sometimes it was confusing because the language was highly technical, such as when they used medical terms in discussions of carcinogenic substances. Yet it opened my eyes to the fact that there was more to safety than just immediate physical threats on the job site. Long-term general health was equally important.

There are all kinds of hidden dangers on a work site, including cancer-causing chemicals, and workers must be trained to recognize and deal with these. Taking a cue from the lessons learned at the board, our training centre set up special classes to teach workers how to recognize and handle hazardous components on a job site. Ontario later made this kind of training mandatory under the Workplace Hazardous Materials Information System (WHMIS) legislation.

The director of the Canadian Occupational Centre for Health and Safety was Dr. Gordon Atherley who later introduced me to a Swedish doctor in charge of the occupational program in Sweden. In turn, I was invited to visit the Construction Trades Occupational Health Centres in Sweden in the fall of 1988. I brought with me Carmen Principato, the manager of Local 506, and Joe Mancinelli from Hamilton, son of Enrico (Henry) Mancinelli, vice-president of the Laborer's Union in Canada.

In Sweden, I was impressed by two programs: the ergonomic program, and the rehabilitation clinic for back injury in Sundsvall, Sweden. I learned that straight shovels with straight handles are illegal in Sweden. All of them must be curved to diminish the stress on the back. They also designed and built small lightweight folding chairs to be attached to the calf which allowed a cement finisher or tile setter to sit while working, thus neutralizing back stress. The Swedish approach to back injury was the opposite to the practice in Ontario where most doctors prescribed rest and pills. In Sweden, they took an aggressive approach and sent injured workers immediately to a rehabilitation program. The clinic in Sundsvall was dedicated to back injuries.

Impressed by what I had seen in Sweden, I initially allocated space and hired a full-time instructor to teach our members how to prevent back injuries. Ultimately I wanted to set up a laboratory to analyze and modify the working tools to be more worker-friendly. Unfortunately, I ran out of time and my successors, for whatever reasons, did not follow through. I still believe that tool modification is necessary to prevent or at least minimize injuries.

Also unfulfilled was my dream of a rehabilitation clinic. I had dedicated an entire floor of the new building to a rehabilitation clinic and a Swedish doctor helped us with the layout, including a walking track. However, nothing was done after I left.

By the end of the 1980s, we had about a thousand retired members. These were the Local 183 builders who had fought many of the battles to build a great union. We remembered their contributions by creating a retirees' club in the new building, complete with a space equipped with billiards, card tables and, of course, a good espresso coffee machine. We also hired a full-time person, Sal Principato, to look after their needs, help them with their pensions, and to run recreational programs. We expanded our trust fund to include pensioners and, for a reduced monthly premium, they were covered for prescription drugs (some retired younger than sixty-five), dental care, hearing aids, vision care, reduced life insurance, and other benefits. I have to say, since I have myself become a beneficiary of the retirees' plan, it is excellent.

The new building was not just a monument to our history, it was also designed as a living, breathing exemplar of our everyday mantra—to best serve our members. The new facility opens many doors, literally and figuratively, in that regard. We were not the first to initiate free legal services but we were first to do it in house.

During the 1989–90 negotiations we included a five-cents-an-hour contribution to our newly created trust fund to provide free legal services, jointly administered with employers. We carved out some space in the new complex for a number of full-time lawyers and paralegals. The free plan did not cover everything but did offer help with personal real estate transactions (buying a home or renewing a mortgage), assistance with problems related to immigration, help with uncontested divorces, and initial consultation on a variety of other issues.

As I noted earlier, the building complex was conceived as a hub to serve our members and by extension the trade union movement as a whole, which brings me to my next point. There were many halls of fame dedicated to businessmen, artists, and sports players, but there was no hall of fame for the trade unionists who dedicated their lives to the betterment of Canadian workers. Many of them accomplished outstanding achievements and in so doing improved not only workers' lives but also the quality of life of all Canadians. I asked myself many times why the Canadian labour movement had never initiated a hall of fame to honour these outstanding Canadians and then I decided to take the initiative to honour workers' champions.

I consulted with Professor Desmond Morton, a respected Canadian historian, as well as with representatives from the Canadian Labour Congress, the Ontario Federation of Labour, and the Toronto Labour Council to sit on the board of governors of a Canadian Labour Hall of Fame. The CLC nominated President Shirley Carr, the OFL sent its president, Gord Wilson, and the Toronto Labour Council offered its president, Linda Torney. I added some representatives from our locals and the Ontario district council.

We agreed that we would hold a ceremony annually to honour new inductees, preferably around Labour Day. We would ask Canadian labour organizations to submit nominations for candidates. We stipulated that eligible candidates should either be deceased or not have been active in the labour movement for the past seven years, in order to eliminate any politics. With the exception of the first round of inductees, the number of new annual inductees would be no more than five. We decided to induct the following people in that first year: Evelyn Armstrong, John W. Bruce, Gerry Gallagher, Helena Gutteridge, Claude Jodoin, James Bryson McLachan, Charles Millard, Daniel O'Donoghue, Madeleine Parent, and Robert Russell.

We commissioned a painted portrait of each inductee. The initial induction took place at the same time as the opening ceremony of our new building. Premier Bob Rae cut the official ribbon. The following year another commemorative ceremony took place and it seemed that the Labour Hall of Fame would go on as an institution. Strangely, however, after my resignation in 1992, it folded. Such is politics and such is life.

CHAPTER 30

MY LAST STRIKE

In 1990, we managed to renegotiate all our civil engineering collective agreements without a strike, except for one in the sewer and water-main sector. The spokesman for that employers' association was Remo Bandiera, owner of a family company with the same name. Remo was a corpulent, bright person. The two of us had clashed in the late 1960s after I had certified his company because he refused to deduct monthly dues on the grounds that his employees did not want to pay what they were required to pay under the collective agreement. I filed a grievance and took it all the way to arbitration. He had a lawyer and Reilly and I spoke for the union. We won.

In 1988, Remo replaced Fred De Gasperis as spokesman for the sewer and water-main contractors' association after a tentative settlement I hammered out with Fred was rejected by the association. I remember Remo coming to my office in his new role. He juggled the amounts I had agreed upon with Fred, lowering the initial increase but adding more during the life of the agreement.

"Remo" I said, "the package is higher than before you started messing with it."

"Yes, I know," replied Remo. "But this is my settlement!"

I had to laugh. Remo was an able operator and over the years he had helped a lot of small contractors, thus ensuring their loyalty. Small and medium companies were the majority in the association but they employed the minority of employees. Assisting Remo was young Mike McNally, who had started his own tunneling company. Mike was the toughest of them all and both Remo and Mike strongly believed in management rights and saw the union as an intrusion into their business.

Remo, in 1990, adopted the classic strategy of divide and conquer. He settled with the Operating Engineers Local 793 but forced us to strike by proposing a second-class settlement. All of our members complied with our strike action but a number of small companies were able to carry on working with just their foremen and other management employees on the job. This was not difficult for small contractors since their key employees were the operating engineers.

Our members were demoralized to see their companies continue to operate. They were used to a total shutdown of all projects during our strikes. After a few weeks, the complaints from our members grew too loud for comfort. At the weekly Sunday meeting, I explained that it did not really matter that small companies were still working because the impact was small. In fact, in the big picture, it was negligible. The only reason that they were still working was to demoralize us. After all, I told them, all big companies were shut down tight. My arguments were to no avail. From the members' perspective, a strike was a strike and nobody should have been working.

The following Monday morning about 7 a.m., I called Frank Giles, president of Operating Engineers Local 793.

"Frank," I said, "why won't your members respect our picket lines?"

"Call your friend Joe," Frank replied, referring to Joe Kennedy, the manager of Local 793.

"I tried," I said, "but Joe does not answer. You have the authority if you want to do it. I know that your members are legally bound to cross our picket line but over many years we have always supported each other."

"Fine," Frank replied. "At noon I will personally go to the picket lines and tell our members to stop working."

"At noon?" I said. "Why the hell don't you go now!"

"First I have to bury my mother in law," he said. "As soon as the funeral is over I will go."

Needless to say, I was speechless.

Frank kept his word. At noon he went from job to job and stopped his Operating Engineers. The association was ready for it and the next day, Tuesday, filed a cease-and-desist order at the Ontario Labour Relations Board against the Operating Engineers Local 793. The hearing was set for the following day, a Wednesday. The board is very speedy in dealing with applications regarding an illegal strike or lockout and its decisions are usually immediate, that is, the day of the hearing.

Representing Local 793 was Al Minsky who put up a brilliant defence, and there was no decision of the board that night. Of course, I don't know what he said because I wasn't there, but it must have been a robust argument because we bought more time. We met the next day, Thursday, at the Constellation Hotel at the request of the government conciliation officers. We made no progress and decided to meet again on the following day, Friday. In the meantime, there was still no decision by the Labour Board, which was highly unusual. Again, we met all day on Friday with no real progress.

After supper on that last day I came up with a strategy and called Reilly to tell him to call Remo and say I went home sick. Then he was to make a direct appeal, saying: "Look, Remo, you have the opportunity to settle with me now if you want. On Monday you will face Stefanini again and you know how stubborn he is!"

Reilly was to present him with a new off-the-record proposal which, while lower than our last official offer, was still above our rock-bottom-deal point. I told Reilly that Remo would come back with a counter offer that could be lower than our offer but not by much. It would be "Remo's offer," which I knew from my previous dealings with him was important to him. He needed to feel that it was his settlement, that he owned it.

What Remo and Reilly did not know was that I had had a number of off-the-record meetings with the bigger players and we had agreed to a fair settlement. However, they were being out-voted by the small and medium-sized contractors who held the majority and thus deadlocked the bargaining. In the years to come, the association applied for accreditation at the Labour Board where the voting rules were changed so that it was no longer one vote per company but a number of votes based on the number of hours worked by their employees. This effectively stopped the tail from wagging the dog.

At about 1 a.m., Reilly called me at home. Everything went exactly as expected. The tentative settlement was ratified by our members through a secret ballot. A couple of weeks later I heard the rest of the story. Remo had been waiting for a decision from the Labour Board. By Friday night, he was convinced that the association had lost its case at the Board so he took my bait. The board, in fact, had ruled in favour of Remo and against Local 793. The decision was sent to the association's lawyer Friday at 4:30 p.m. and their lawyer called the association office but, it being a Friday, the offices had closed at 4 p.m. "God is on our side," I said when I learned of this sequence of events. If the association had known of the Labour Board's decision, chances are its holy war would have carried on and who knows what the result might have been. Perhaps our image of invincibility would have been shattered.

It must be said that over the years we enjoyed a fair to good relationship with the sewer and water-main contractors' association. It was led by fair employers such as Jim Valentine, D. McNally, Stan and Peter Collini, Paul Golini, Domenic Alfieri, and later by Fred De Gasperis. When I announced my retirement it was the stern Mike McNally, much to my surprise, who called me for the first and only time. He said, quite earnestly, that he would be sorry to see me go and added that there had never been anything personal.

He was fighting for his rights just as I, of course, had always fought for our members' rights.

CHAPTER 31

LUNCH WITH
THE POLICE

A round the end of September 1990, Chester De Toni and I had lunch with the labour squads of both the Toronto Police Service and the Peel Police Service, at the Burgundy Room of the Constellation Hotel. These were special police units whose job it was to know the structure of both the employers' businesses and the trade unions in the GTA; and to understand the laws and how conflicts arose both between unions over jurisdiction, and between employers and unions during certification or contract negotiations. They were also tasked with keeping tabs on any outside influences, such as organized crime groups which may have interests in the construction industry on both sides of the employer-employee fence.

The lunch was an annual ritual, a treat for the police labour squads reflecting our intention to keep things cordial. It was our policy to co-operate with them and coordinate our strike actions. Before putting up a picket line on any project we would inform the appropriate labour squad the day before, letting them know the location and any other planned action.

The policy paid off. The police, who are unionized themselves, had changed their attitude towards strikes since those confrontational days in the 1960s. By the 1990s, they were co-operative and supportive, as long as we respected the law. Over the years, experience and changing attitudes taught me to change tactics and adapt, doing away with flying squads and, instead, using just a couple of picketers. It was much more effective.

I remember a contractor who called the police at the mere sight of our picket lines. He was told, "It is their right to be there, unless they commit any unlawful act." Of course, in that case we had called the police the day before to let them know our plans. In my many years of directing a multitude of strikes involving thousands of workers I can boast that not one of our members was ever arrested for something done during picket duty and much of that was down to good communications with the police.

De Toni, who had returned to our local shortly after he left in 1971, organized the lunch. He was a very sociable person who liked good food and wine and loved entertaining. I can honestly say everybody liked Chester, including the police. We were joined by Detective Danny James from the intelligence squad, a well-known police officer whom we liked and had learned to respect since we first met during the concrete forming showdown. Our dealings with him were almost on a collegial basis.

In 1984, I had called Danny complaining about the way I had been treated by two Peel Regional Police detectives. I had been conducting a province-wide negotiation at the Skyline Hotel near the airport, which is in Peel's jurisdiction. I called my office as I usually did to check for messages before it closed for the evening. This was long before digital voice mail and cell phones. My secretary said two police detectives wanted to speak to me urgently and I told her to let them know that I would be available after the dinner break. Accordingly, two detectives came to the Skyline Hotel around 7 p.m. and we met.

One of the detectives asked me what I was doing with Paul Volpe on Sunday, November 13, 1983. Volpe was a well-known mobster who had been murdered and found in the trunk of his car in the vicinity of the airport, not far from our offices, on November 14, 1983. He was last seen by a witness leaving a Woodbridge café and the case is unsolved to this day. At the time, it was a hot story. I thought the detective was joking because I did not have any dealings with Volpe. I replied, "I thought he was with you that day."

The detective asked me the same question, a second time, my answer was the same. He got quite upset and in an angry tone told me that if I did not answer the question they would take me to the police station. I realized he was serious and I thought for a minute and said, "He could not have been with me that day as I was with the Pope."

The detective got even angrier with me, thinking I was winding him up but, in fact, it was true. On November 13, I was at a special ceremony in Saint Peter's Basilica in Rome for the beatification of a saint. I had been there together with Wally Majesky, president of the Toronto Labour Council, as guests of an Italian trade union. The Italian union could not arrange an audience on such short notice but it was able to get us invited to the special mass. My seat assignment was number 11, around the altar, very close to the Pope.

The detectives wanted me to sign a statement that was full of incorrect notes. I refused and called Danny James the following day to complain about the treatment. He laughed and said not to worry about it. This was an example of how my so-called friends in the labour movement had tried to eliminate me as a rival. They either did not realize or forgot that I was away in Rome that week.

A few days after that encounter Danny visited me at my office and said he had been the one to open the trunk of the car to find Volpe's body stuffed inside in the fetal position.

He said his first thought was: "Fuck, there goes my overtime!" Then he added: "If you tell anyone I said that I'll deny it."

At the end of our lunch, I brought up an issue which had bothered me for some time. A few years earlier, a United Food and Commercial Workers International Union representative had told me that I was "under electronic surveillance." This was disturbing. He said he got the tip from a police officer who had a cottage next to him and over the years they had become friends. While it was uncomfortable to think about, I did not get too excited because everything I did was above board. I ran a clean ship.

A couple of years earlier, I had fired one of our representatives when staff told me he was trying to peddle drugs in the office. After we fired him he was hired by a trust fund and his compensation package included a car. The car was used during a gas station robbery and the administrator of the trust was notified but the representative in question claimed it was stolen from him four days before the robbery and that he had not bothered to report the theft. The administrator also discovered that the man had used the fund's credit card to purchase personal items worth up to $4,000. The administrator complained to police, who said, "Don't worry, we will look after everything." Nothing happened.

My own suspicion was that the ex-representative had been turned into a police informant, although I would question how valuable any information he offered could be. I put it bluntly to Danny James, "If you want to know what is going on with our union you are welcome to have a full-time officer in our office and we will fully co-operate with him, but we object that a drug addict, scum of the earth, is being used against us. These people will tell you anything but the truth."

There was a prolonged silence; then Danny said in a low voice, "Sometimes we have no choice but to use those individuals."

After lunch, Chester drove home with one of the police officers, an older man, who noted during the ride, "Danny did not deny anything. John must be right."

I think the police spend so much time investigating organized crime that they expect to find it everywhere, which is a short-sighted approach, certainly in our case. For example, after my retirement I was involved in a labour venture fund. We were considering a proposed investment and while doing our due diligence I met with a former OPP officer. As we talked about my encounters with other police officers in my career he nodded and said, "You were always surrounded by sharks but the police did not understand why or how you survived. They wanted to find out who was protecting you."

The simple truth is that no one was protecting me. Maybe they should have given me more credit?

CHAPTER 32

THE NEW ONTARIO GOVERNMENT, 1990

No one expected the NDP and Bob Rae to win the election in 1990. This was good news for our local because we had a good relationship with Rae and we were one of the few construction unions which remitted monthly contributions to the NDP. Given the nature of politics at the local union level, we donated based on a candidate-by-candidate choice, according to their merits and their commitment to our cause, which was primarily job creation and social justice. Sometimes it was just because they were candidates of outstanding quality. At election time we sent out a number of union representatives to help campaign.

Rae had been a federal MP before jumping to the Ontario NDP in 1982 and winning the party's leadership that year. That same year he was elected as an MPP, and in 1985 he was instrumental in helping the Ontario Liberals form a government after the Progressive Conservatives failed to win a majority. In the 1982 election, we had sent two representatives to help Bob Rae's campaign in York South. One of those was John Colacci who reported back that Rae was in trouble. So without telling Rae or his campaign manager, I assigned a dozen representatives to the riding because, in my opinion, we needed a person like Rae in the Ontario legislature. He won comfortably with 45 per cent of the votes, well ahead of Liberal John Nunziata who took 35 per cent.

In 1990 the coalition's term came to an end and a new election was called for October. Ten days before the election, Bob Rae invited me to lunch at a Yorkville Italian restaurant. I brought one of our full-time lawyers, Dan McCarthy, a Jesuit priest who had left the order to study law and marry. He was a truly outstanding person. I often enjoyed talking to him on a multitude of political, historical, and social issues.

At the lunch I warned Rae about the upcoming economic crisis. Rae was incredulous but I was witnessing serious cracks in the building industry and I was paying attention to the many warnings builders were giving me. I strongly believe that the construction industry is a barometer of the national economy and that it can forecast good or bad trends. As it happened, once Rae was elected he inherited a mess nobody was prepared for. Many big builders went out of business and the value of real estate fell by half. Few had the acumen to ride out the storm. Those who got out ahead of it included men like De Gasperis and Muzzo who wisely cut loose their riskier investments. They took losses but kept their more promising ventures. Their foresight paid off handsomely while other building giants, such as Bramalea Developments, disappeared.

Among the many new programs instituted by Rae was the Premier's Economic Advisory Council. It was composed of leaders of industry, academics, labour, and government and I was one of the four labour leaders on the body. The council met once a month and Premier Rae was always present. Before every meeting we took delivery at our homes of thick binders with all the background for the issues to be discussed.

Among those highly knowledgeable financial and economic gurus who comprised the council, I felt like a fish out of water. My knowledge of the economy was superficial but I quickly realized some important things. I learned, for example, that a provincial government, however good its intentions, could not do much to change economic reality. There were too many external factors, not least a global recession at the time. At best, a provincial government can create favourable conditions for business expansion when the broader economy turns around.

Another realization I had involved the public debt. This is different from the deficit. A deficit is a shortfall in a budget year. It is money which is not covered by revenues from taxes and fees and so the government must borrow to cover its spending in that year. The debt is the accumulation of all those deficits. Year after year, deficit budgets add to the debt and that debt carries interest which again, adds to the deficit, which adds to the debt. It is surprising how many citizens either do not know about our public debt, or do not care. Unless it is controlled, government debt is like a cancer that grows year after year and can destroy the economic stability of a nation. We have just to look at a number of European countries, or even Detroit across the border from Ontario, to see the consequences. We are fooling ourselves if we think it cannot happen here.

At the Premier's Council, I promoted construction projects and in particular the new Highway 407 as an important component of our provincial infrastructure connecting many manufacturing enterprises in the Golden Horseshoe area. It would bypass the congestion of Highway 401 to the south and create thousands of jobs.

Bob Rae's government was unfairly criticized for the economic recession which hit the province about the time he was elected. It hit hard just at the moment he took power. There was nothing he could have done to prevent it.

I recall an occasion when the advisory council members were asked by Premier Rae to forward suggestions for topics he might include in a live televised speech he was going to deliver. Dan McCarthy and I prepared some ideas we thought were worthy of consideration. McCarthy polished them up and sent them in. As it turned out, some of our ideas made it into Rae's text. The speech was quite a big deal because it was unheard of for the Ontario Premier to go on television to give what was essentially a "state of the province" address. The following morning, McCarthy came to my office jubilantly claiming credit for some of the content of the premier's speech. We were thrilled because the Rae government was very important to Local 183. At the time, when there was very little residential construction going on Rae vigorously promoted the building of non-profit and affordable housing which in turn kept many of our members working.

The Rae government also tabled and passed labour legislation which was extremely favourable to union workers. One piece of legislation greatly affected our building maintenance members, including cleaners, who often were the first services that management would sublet to non-union companies. Rae changed the law so that a union was certified for the location and not just for the company. As a result, if work was sublet, it had to be given to a union shop.

The government was generally receptive to our ideas. For example, I remember one day when senior staff at the Industrial Standards Branch of the Ministry of Labour invited me to meet and said the premier had asked for suggestions on how to update and improve the regulations around labour laws. I was caught by surprise but managed to come up with two suggestions. One, compensation for unpaid wages owed to employees in the event that a company folded and went out of business. This happened a lot among "fly by night" contractors in the construction sector. Second, a reduction in the standard workweek for roads, sewer and water-main construction. The director strongly argued against the first idea, saying it would only be more incentive for companies not to pay employees. I countered by saying the government should make the companies' directors personally liable, and it carried the day. As a result, Ontario has the Wage Protection Act covering unpaid wages up to $2,500. Unfortunately, I did not win over the director on the workweek issues.

Rae was always being accused of being anti-business which I thought was unfair and untrue. While I can only speak for the construction industry, I do have an anecdote which suggests otherwise. Fred De Gasperis called me to meet him at his office when he was part of a development group building a huge residential complex called Springdale between Brampton and Toronto. The development meant thousands of jobs for our members but progress had ground to a halt because of a dispute with the Region of Peel over the building of schools. Without schools, the builders could not build. The root problem was a fight between the region and the province. Peel wanted money from the province to build schools but the province refused, saying if it gave in to Peel it would have to give in to every other municipality. It was a recession and money was tight.

Fred asked me to speak to Premier Rae about the matter and I did. In response, he created a new office called the Construction Facilitator's Office and appointed to it Dale Martin, a former City of Toronto councillor who was well versed in municipal politics. I still do not know how Dale managed to do it but he resolved the issue and the green light was given to build thousands of homes. The day Rae's Minister of Municipal Affairs, David S. Cooke, stood up in the legislature to announce the creation of the Construction Facilitator's Office I was invited to sit in the visitors' gallery with the president of the Ontario Home Builders Association and then Metro Councillor Howard Moscoe, who was also president of the Federation of Canadian Municipalities. We were asked to stand and we received loud applause from all the MPPs. That was on April 9, 1992.

The Rae government did a lot for Local 183. I regret that after I left, in the next provincial election, Local 183's new management supported another political party.

CHAPTER 33

THE PEACE TREATIES

The organizing activities of Local 183 in what some considered the exclusive jurisdictions of craft unions as well as in the industrial, commercial, and institutional sector were always controversial among other labour groups. The Toronto Building and Construction Trades Council often attacked us over our presence in ICI. Fortunately, most of the other trades, such as plumbers and painters, were not affected by the disputes and they remained either neutral or on our side. The reason why some were on our side was primarily self-interest. We were the real power in the residential sector. They knew that they needed our support in the event of a strike or for organizing assistance in the residential sector.

For example, in 1985 the United Association of Plumbers and Steamfitters Local 46 had a strike in the residential housing sector. Sean O'Ryan, the dynamic and progressive young business manager of the plumbers, called asking for our help. I did not hesitate and assigned a full-time representative, Quinto Ceolin, to O'Ryan. I told Quinto to make sure our guys respected the plumbers' picket lines, and eventually O'Ryan won the strike and his local established strong roots in the residential sector.

O'Ryan developed an organizing strategy that he called "sectoral organizing." It included six months of "marketing" their union to the non-union plumbers working in hundreds of subdivisions throughout Southern Ontario. He then invited the workers to the Triumph Hotel on Keele Street for a one-evening signup event. Four hundred non-union plumbers joined the union for one dollar that night and within the next three days they signed up another hundred, thereby capturing 80 per cent of the low-rise plumbing workforce in the region.

O'Ryan was then in a tough battle with twenty or so contractors for a first agreement and his members had to go on strike for seven weeks before reaching a settlement. Sean has often stated that "their organizing program and negotiation for a first agreement could not have been such a success without the support and assistance of John Stefanini and Local 183." To this day, Local 46 enjoys a 95 per cent market share in the residential sector. O'Ryan went on to a stellar career in the union and was promoted to be senior administrative assistant to the president of the Plumbers International in Washington.

The climax of our difficulties with the other trades came in 1988. At that time, the manager of the Toronto Building and Construction Trade Council was Dave Johnson who was a member of Ironworkers Local 721. He fought us tooth and nail. He did not do so out of malice. As a matter of fact, I know that he respected Local 183. He simply felt it was right to protect the jurisdiction of an affiliate craft union.

He brought a case in court claiming our agreement with builders contravened the master agreement of the Toronto Building and Construction Trades Council. The day of the court ruling coincided with the Trades Council's monthly evening meetings. The court ruling was such that, upon first reading, it gave the impression of giving the Toronto Building and Construction Trades Council a victory, especially in the first part of the judgment. Later in the afternoon, however, our lawyer Ray Koskie called me and explained that the court ruling had actually come down on our side.

That evening I went to the monthly meeting of the trades council, something I rarely did. At the meeting Johnson was beaming over the ruling and claiming the court had vindicated his position. I brought the decision with me, fresh from the Koskie briefing. I explained to those in attendance that, in fact, the decision said the opposite of what Johnson was describing. Quite understandably, Johnson became upset, banging his fist on the table and saying he had had enough. A few days later, he quit his job. I regretted his resignation because, apart from our differences in this matter, he was a good manager.

The battle continued. Both the carpenters and the ironworkers brought complaints against us at the Ontario Labour Relations Board, accusing us of violating the single-trade province-wide bargaining legislation. To make things worse, at the same time a major dispute broke out between us and the Operating Engineers Local 793. The latter was a problem which had been simmering for a long time over the operation of small excavating equipment, the so-called Tonka Toys, in the utility industry.

These mini-excavators, like Bobcats, were operated from time to time by working foremen who were Local 183 members. Joe Kennedy of Operating Engineers Local 793 was extremely protective of his jurisdiction and he was furious at what he saw as an incursion by our union. It did not matter to him how small or how easy it was to operate the Tonka Toys, he claimed any machinery had to be piloted by his members, period. For our part, we resented his inflexible position, especially since the utility sector had been originally organized by us and we had more or less gifted his Local 793 the heavy equipment operators. They gained members without having to lift a finger.

Also, our members had been operating these small excavators ever since they first started to appear on construction sites in the late 1960s and early 1970s. They are compact and can be fitted with a front claw or a bucket and even a small dozer-like blade. They are easy to operate, they get into small places, and they take the hard labour out of site work. Kennedy sent us a written notice of Local 793's intention to withdraw from a forming council his local had set up with ours. This was bad news for us. As a consequence of a variety of earlier jurisdictional agreements, we needed this forming council to remain active in ICI projects.

This was just the beginning of a bitter dispute between us and Local 793. Al Minsky, our lawyer, also acted for Kennedy's local. He was friendly to both parties and he was upset at the situation because it was awkward for him and affected his ability to serve both clients. He invited Joe Kennedy and me to dinner at the Mastro restaurant on Wilson Avenue where he cautioned us that our squabble was detrimental to both organizations and reminded us how much progress we had made by working together. Kennedy acknowledged his points but emphasized in a lengthy speech how sacrosanct his jurisdiction was to him.

I had brought with me two souvenirs from a trip to Edmonton. They were wooden miniatures, one of a tomahawk axe and the other of a peace pipe. After Kennedy made his big speech, I simply pulled the items from my jacket pocket and laid them on the table and said: "Joe, it is up to you. Which do you want to pick up?"

I said nothing more. Kennedy was surprised at my move. He kept quiet for a while and then broke out in a laugh. The two of us hugged. Joe withdrew his notice of withdrawal from the forming council. Minsky was pleased: his mission was accomplished.

We still faced the complaint of the carpenters and ironworkers before the Ontario Labour Relations Board. The day of that hearing, there were fourteen interested parties present. The chair was Rosalie Abella, who would go on to be the youngest Ontario Family Court Judge in Canadian history, at age twenty-nine and, ultimately, in 2004, a member of the Supreme Court of Canada.

One of the delegates from the forming association, Italo Cirone, a forming contractor, asked her for more time to locate a lawyer. Abella was not buying it, noting there had been ample notice and that she had difficulty understanding why his organization could not have retained legal counsel before the hearing.

"With all due respect," Cirone replied, "just take a look around this room and you will see every labour lawyer has already been engaged."

Loud laughter ensued. Indeed, there were some fourteen parties to the dispute, including unions and contractors, all of them represented by counsel. It was a big issue in the industry and their presence underscored its importance.

Then the game began. There was some fascinating legal manoeuvering by the lawyers on the merit or the lack of merit in the complaint against us. After a break, Chair Abella wisely recommended we all sit down and talk this out rather than go through a lengthy and expensive hearing. She offered to appoint a Labour Relations Board officer as facilitator and, in the interests of fair play and being reasonable, I was the first to accept. The others had little choice but to agree.

Over the next few months there was nothing but acrimony during the talks. We broke it down into individual meetings, that is, Local 183 and the carpenters, and Local 183 and the ironworkers. With the ironworkers, the dispute was only around high-rise forming but with the carpenters there was also the residential housing sector. I wanted to find a way to connect everyone so that we could reach common ground.

At one time, Local 183 represented employees of Frost Fence, a subsidiary of Stelco Steel. Stelco had apparently called their chain-link fencing company after the American poet Robert Frost, who in his 1914 poem "Mending Wall" said, "good fences make good neighbours." While the poet actually questions fences for the sake of fences, that line was all I needed to make my point and that is exactly what I said to the Ironworkers Local 721: "Good fences make good neighbours. Why don't we put a fence around ICI for us and we will fence you out from residential?"

It was a deal. We withdrew from ICI and they allowed us to represent rod men for residential construction, something unheard of in North America. I was surprised because I thought the ironworkers would be more difficult than the carpenters. The business manager of the Ironworkers' Local 721 was Al MacIsaac, a trade unionist who was tougher than nails. But Al was realistic. In making the deal he gave up nothing and gained jobs in ICI. We gave up good jobs and in turn we got security and respect.

With the carpenters it took longer although we eventually sorted out our differences thanks to new leadership from Jimmy Smith, John Cartwright, Cosmo Mannella, Tony Iannuzzi, and Ucal Powell. We dealt with the high-rise sector by building a fence in the same manner as we had done with the ironworkers but in residential housing we retained framing and recognized the carpenters' union to represent the finish carpenters and, further, to help each other to organize the unorganized.

The signing of this peace treaty took place at the Constellation Hotel in 1991. Brian Foote, representing the Toronto Construction Association, was so happy he bought six bottles of Dom Pérignon champagne to celebrate. Everybody was pleased, including the Ministry of Labour. I forwarded copies of those unique "peace treaties" to our International and Arthur E. Coia called to congratulate me on them.

"Arthur," I said, "you are the only one who called to recognize what we have achieved. No other international union representative in Canada called."

"I know, they are jealous of what you have managed to accomplish," he replied.

Arthur E. Coia was an extraordinary man. Sadly, he died shortly after I retired. I went to his funeral in Providence, Rhode Island. I was paying my respects at the casket when I turned to greet and offer sympathies to his son, Arthur A. Coia, who was then general president of the union.

"John, my father would have done anything for you," he said as we shook hands.

CHAPTER 34

THE RESCUE OF THE BRICKLAYERS

In the fall of 1990 Chester De Toni asked me to help rescue a Bricklayer's Union known as the Independent Bricklayer Union Local 1. Chester was a friend of the local president, John Meiorin and, in that organization, president was the top position. The Independent Bricklayers Union Local 1 was the former Local 40 of the Bricklayers International Union. Sometime in the late 1960s, it had broken away from the International and formed its own organization. It represented close to 2,000 bricklayers and labourers.

In many ways, the bricklayers were in a perfect position to organize any trade or sector of the construction industry. Being independent, they did not have to pay the monthly per capita to an international union, which in some cases can be onerous. They could also make their own decisions without fear of being contradicted by the parent organization. They nevertheless limited their activities to the trade they represented. The shortcomings of their independent position became clear in the event of a strike. They could not depend on any other trade union's support.

When Chester came to me, the Independent Bricklayers Union Local 1 was in a legal strike position. Its agreement had expired in the spring and the economic realities in the residential industry were rapidly deteriorating to a point where a strike would have been suicidal. Ontario labour law specifies that if a labour organization does not take strike action within six months and if there is no bargaining between parties for more than six months, the union can be decertified as the bargaining agent.

I was not too anxious to get involved. There was a very bitter relationship between Meiorin, the local president, and the employers' association with whom he had to negotiate, and I had enough problems of my own. Nonetheless, De Toni organized a lunch with Meiorin who explained his problems and blamed everything on the employers. I then met the employers who blamed everything on Meiorin for being unrealistic and inflexible. At this point, I was even more reluctant to get involved.

I met the employers' association once again and put the basic question on the table: "What will it take to settle this dispute?"

Two of their conditions were that they only would deal with me, and that they wanted the bricklayers to become affiliated with Local 183. I consulted with Arthur A. Coia during a Florida conference and he told me, off the record: "Sure, go ahead and see what you can do."

I met again with Meiorin who, without hesitation, said he would step back and give me full authority. He added that the survival of his union was more important than his personal role. I met once more with the employers and worked out a tentative settlement for a one-year period. There were some adjustments but overall it did not represent a step backward as originally demanded by the contractors. The one-year term was to give us room to find a more appropriate solution.

The next step was for our tentative understanding to be formalized at the negotiating table by the bricklayers and the employers. Unfortunately, the conciliation officers at the Ministry of Labour scheduled the talks on a day on which I had to travel to Edmonton for pipeline negotiations. I instructed De Toni on every detail of the tentative agreement and advised him on what moves to make during negotiations.

On my return from Edmonton late on a Friday night, De Toni called to tell me that everything had gone up in smoke. I was furious and disappointed at the same time and demanded an explanation. He said, "Meiorin and the contractors started to insult each other and scream at each other and I could not carry on."

The following day, Saturday morning, I started to pick up the pieces. In short order I was able to get an official memorandum of settlement signed and approved by both parties along the same lines as the tentative agreement. The Independent Bricklayers Union Local 1 became part of our Local 183. Another 2,000 members were added to our ranks.

For me, it was poetry. I have already compared the building of our union to the bricklayer's craft, laying one brick on top of the other. We built worker by worker, contractor by contractor, trade by trade to become the largest and strongest construction local of any trade union in Canada and the largest local of the Labourers International anywhere in North America.

CHAPTER 35

THE LABRADOR TRAGEDY

L ife is full of highs and lows and while the early 1990s had some moments of achievement, there were also sad times. In the spring of 1991, I was re-elected by acclamation as the business manager of Local 183 for a four-year term and in August of that year I was also re-elected by acclamation as business manager of the Ontario District Council for another four-year term. Both the local and the council were the largest units of their kind in the International. The day of my re-election at the District Council I left for Goose Bay, Labrador, with our pension fund manager, Onorio D'Agostini and Chester De Toni, a Local 183 representative. I remember feeling down, despite my re-elections.

Part of it was that one of the candidates on my slate for the executive board was not elected. This was not a big political problem for me since I had a solid majority on the executive board and there was mutual respect between myself and the person elected who was not on my slate. What really bothered me was being double-crossed by a local that I had trusted completely and whose vote was crucial. The ballots were secret but it was not too hard to figure out who had betrayed me. I was disgusted at their political games. A friend is a friend and a true friend does not betray another. If they had come out in the open and declared their intention prior to the election, it would have been a different story.

While we were at the airport waiting for our flight, I expressed my feelings to D'Agostini, who was sympathetic but, as he saw things, it was now in the past and we had to move forward. We were heading east at the invitation of Pat McCormack, the business manager of the Newfoundland and Labrador Laborer's Local and we were to join two Laborers International union representatives from the New England area.

Pat had organized a fishing trip on the Eagle River in Labrador, which is famous for brook trout and salmon and fly fishing. We flew from Toronto to Goose Bay and then boarded a small turbo plane to get to the lodge, about one hour away. Looking out the window at the landscape it struck me how desolate it was. There was not a single house or road in that wilderness. We arrived in the late afternoon on a Friday and immediately headed for the river. We struck out.

The lodge guides recommended we move to a higher location by another small lodge. They said salmon would be resting up there after clearing the rapids and we would have better luck. We needed to leave very early in the morning so we hit the sack and tried to get some sleep.

Unfortunately, I did not sleep well. I was sharing a room with my friend Chester and he was snoring like a chainsaw. When dawn broke I was a bit relieved to see it was raining heavily. I was hoping we would cancel and that I could go back to bed and catch up on my sleep. The guides, however, were certain the rain was going to end soon so we packed up and got ready to move upstream. It was an unusually warm day and we were wearing raincoats, which made hiking up the hills uncomfortable. Crossing the river was itself an adventure since the far side was full of big boulders and slippery to negotiate.

I did not know why but I had an ominous feeling. I thought it might be something left over from the re-election issue. It was definitely something negative. I told the guide how I felt and he said I should just take my time getting to the ridge and he hung back with me. There were another two guides, one with the Americans who were farther ahead, the other with Chester and Onorio.

The uphill trail was slippery and tricky, and the forest was thick. The trail had been built simply by clearing pines to create a path and over time rain had eroded the ground around the tree roots. We had to be careful where we walked so as not to get caught in the holes between the roots.

I took my time climbing with my guide and about halfway up we met Chester and Onorio resting with their guide. We joined them for a few minutes but they were off again almost immediately, despite my appeals for them to walk slowly with us.

A few minutes after they left and while we were still resting, D'Agostini came running back saying that Chester was ill. My guide took off like a mountain goat down that difficult trail to reach the base camp and radio for medical support.

I followed D'Agostini up about fifty meters and found my friend Chester on the ground with no vital signs. The guide said he had fallen and died instantly. I said a few prayers over him and moved on to the upper camp. I was dead tired but I felt guilty that I abandoned my friend so I went back to see him. The three guides were busy cutting trees to make space for the helicopter to land. I performed the last rites, although I have no idea whether I performed them correctly or not. I based them on what I remembered of a priest giving them to my mother.

With the heavy rain pouring down, I returned to the upper camp. The weather had deteriorated so much that the helicopter was unable to land. The three guides took Chester's body to a small shelter about a hundred meters away, to protect it from wild animals. Chester was overweight and it was quite an undertaking for the guides to carry his body over such inhospitable terrain.

The following morning the helicopter came. First they took D'Agostini and me to the base camp and then they took Chester's body to St. Anthony, Newfoundland, for an autopsy, which was required under the circumstances. D'Agostini and I returned to Toronto, taking four flights across Labrador and Quebec before getting home.

Before leaving, I told the three guides to visit me in Toronto. In the winter months they came west to work as carpenters. When they arrived, I helped them find employment and I asked them to take a small plaque with them back to Labrador inscribed: "This mountain stream is called 'Chester Stream' in memory of a good man who lost his life here."

It was a small gesture and they were more than happy to do it for me. As far as I know, it is still there.

CHAPTER 36

MY DEPARTURE

Chester De Toni's sudden death was a huge blow which left me even more sad and depressed. It also caused me to reflect on my life. In 1990, my doctor had advised me to change my lifestyle after having my blood analyzed at a specialized laboratory in California. He said the results suggested my risk of death was four times higher than that of the average man of my age.

This would mean a drastic adjustment, especially around my work. To really effect that kind of change I would have to quit my position. I thought about it and discussed it with my family and decided that I had little choice in the matter. The only question was when I would retire.

That same year, Arthur E. Coia had come for dinner at our house and offered me a vice-presidency at the International. He was shocked when I turned him down. That position is the highest that can be aspired to by a Canadian. However, it would have required more traveling, more lunches and dinners, no regular schedule: the opposite of what my doctor had ordered. What Arthur also did not know was that I already made up my mind to quit for health reasons.

After returning from Labrador I went to Las Vegas to attend the International Union's convention, which is held every five years. I was asked to second the nomination of Angelo Fosco for the office of general president which I gladly did. Angelo was good to me over the years. (He also died after I retired. I attended his funeral in Chicago out of respect and in recognition of his co-operation when I was running both the local and the district council.)

As I said, Chester's death played heavily on my heart and mind while I was in Las Vegas. I reflected on my life and realized that I had never stopped to smell the roses. As a young man, I had not gone to parties or dance halls but went from house to house to sign up non-union workers to grow our union. My life had been about conflicts, confrontation, lengthy strikes, dirty politics, the occasional backstabbing, and never-ending stress. It was the double-crossing animosity of my world that bothered me the most.

Let me give you an example. Construction is part of every Italian's DNA. Take a look at the magnificent structures in Italy built from Roman times through the Renaissance to today. For many generations, an Italian immigrant's first priority on landing in Canada was to buy a house. Most of us settled around the Danforth Avenue area in the east end of Toronto and, of course, around College Street, St. Clair, and Eglinton Avenue in the west end. By the 1970s, the majority wanted new and bigger houses with bigger backyards where they could grow more vegetables and tomatoes so they migrated to the four corners of the GTA. A good number choose Vaughan and specifically Woodbridge.

I was tempted to move there, too, but instead I purchased an empty lot in central Etobicoke. In August 1979, after selling the house we had built in 1967, I started construction of my new house. I was the builder and the general contractor and I engaged each trade as I needed. My problem was to find union contractors since at the time the residential housing sector was non-union with the few exceptions of basement contractors and concrete-and-drain crews that had been organized by Local 183.

As the manager of a major construction union, I had no choice but to employ unionized labour. It drove up the cost of the house because some of the contractors I used were primarily ICI and thus were paid a higher rate. All the same, the major expense turned out not to be wages but sabotage. We were almost finished drywalling when the subcontractor complained to me that a door opening was wrong. I checked with the carpenter, a good and experienced man, who looked at it strangely and said, "How the heck did that happen?"

He set about pulling the frame apart and noticed an electrical wire had been cut. By coincidence, an electrician was also on-site and when he came over to look he also became suspicious because it was a clean cut. Usually if an electrical cable is cut by accident it is not a "clean cut" and the tradesman who caused it would report it immediately to the electrician or the site supervisor.

The electrician then tested other electrical circuits and found that all of them were dead. Somebody had cut all the electric wiring. They had been cut clean, with a pair of wire cutters, and then the cut end had been stuffed back into the hole drilled into the two-by-four stud so as to cover up the sabotage. This was no accident. We found many places with cut wires placed back into the hole. Clearly, this was not just deliberate but maliciously calculated. Ironically, if the carpenter had not made a mistake on the door, it would have ruined me. The biggest cost in a house is in the finishing. If the drywalls had been taped, the tiles installed, the walls painted, the wallpaper hung, the finishing electrical fixtures completed, the plumbing installed, and the sabotage found only after all that, I would have been bankrupt. The insurance policy covered me in case of fire, not vandalism.

I had to hire a full-time security guard for overnights and Saturdays and Sundays. Of course, this all cost me money and added to my mortgage. In my opinion, somebody up there made the carpenter make a stupid "mistake" with the door. Everything happens for a reason. This sabotage was another example of how my invisible enemies were trying to harm me. Shortly after this, someone I had considered a friend in the union movement asked me, "How is your house construction going?"

It was a perfectly reasonable question but I had never told him I was building a house. I do not mind a good fight out in the open. I do not like fighting in the dark. I hated that other union leaders would badmouth me and make false reports to Washington that created problems for me. This ignominious practice continued even after my retirement because certain people were obsessed with the idea that I might return in some capacity.

On a personal level, I also felt guilty about how little time I spent with my family. My children, Mark and Lisa, had grown up without all the attention and care a father should give because I put the union cause ahead of my family too often. There was still time to dedicate my attention to my family before becoming an empty nester and so I knew I had to take that opportunity to make things right.

When the International Union's pension fund changed the retirement rules to thirty years of service and out, I decided that it was a good time to go. I was at the peak of my power and there was no real enemy in sight, at least not in the open. I had another three years to go on my mandate, I had considerable power and authority, and politicians at all levels of government were seeking our support. We had truly become a powerhouse. Most unions and employers respected us. I had an army of lawyers, accountants, and dedicated union representatives, good secretarial staff, and the support of the best members in the labour movement.

I am a lover of history. From history I learned the best time to go is at the peak of power. Those who ignore this rule are not remembered as well as those who follow it. The decline comes to all, sooner or later. Early in 1992, I gave notice to the Ontario

District Council that I was resigning, saying that I wanted to dedicate my remaining few months in office to Local Union 183.

It was like a thunderbolt out of the clear blue sky. People were shocked but I had made up my mind. I was fifty-two years old. It had been thirty-three years since I had arrived as an eighteen-year-old boy in Toronto, speaking little English, driven only by a dream of a better life. I had spent my working years building Local 183 and now it was time to move on.

That spring I finalized the renewals of all of the local's agreements. I went over as many details as possible of the local's administration structure and organization to fine-tune everything for my successor. I also had an opportunity to repay Gerry Gallagher's favour in hiring me all those years ago. His widow, Olive, called and asked for help in getting a job as a representative for her son, Michael. He was working as an operating engineer and a member of the Operating Engineers Local 793 so I called my friend Joe Kennedy, the local manager, and took him to lunch.

I asked Joe to hire Mike Gallagher as a personal favour and explained it was very important to me because of the debt I owed his late father. I also told Joe that if he could not do it, I would hire Mike, but I felt he would be better off working in his own union and trade. Joe called me a week later to say he was going to hire Mike and Olive also called to thank me. Years later Mike Gallagher became the manager of the Local 793 of the Operating Engineers.

Before leaving for good I wanted to make my last appearance at the board of trustees for each of the funds we had created. The trust fund, the pension fund, the welfare fund, the vacation-with-pay fund, the prepaid legal fund, and the training fund—all of them, with the exception of the pension plan, I had founded. The only meeting I could not get to was that of the training fund which was not scheduled until October. I decided to wait until then rather than call a special meeting.

On July 24, 1992, they held my retirement dinner and I gave my farewell speech. There were close to a thousand attendees from unions, employers, government offices and other interested parties. At the end the band played "My Way."

In early August, I called a meeting of the local's executive board and I recommended Mike Reilly be appointed to replace me. Reilly had announced his intention to retire but I thought it would be appropriate for him to retire as manager. I had to do some homework ahead of the meeting because the majority of the executive board members were not exactly thrilled at my endorsement. Many people advised me that I was making a mistake. Perhaps I should have listened.

Shortly after my retirement, I went to Israel and Egypt with my wife. On my return I went to the last meeting of the training fund. We were all sitting down, union, employers, and trustees, when Reilly came in. He announced the meeting was not going to take place as long as I was there. Everybody was shocked and speechless. Reilly then called on the union trustees to leave the meeting and though they were union representatives under his direction none of them moved an inch. At the end of the meeting, I resigned as a trustee of the training fund as announced the previous August.

Reilly was not finished, however. He successfully blocked a motion made at a previous meeting which would have named the training centre after me. This despite the fact that the sign had already been made. Then he ordered the removal of all the pictures of me at various events over the years which were hung at the Local 183 headquarters.

I am sad to note that after I left, things went from bad to worse at Local 183. The peace treaties we had worked so hard to sign were often broken and battles with the carpenters flared up again. Within two years, Local 183 was placed under International supervision after a number of scandals appeared in the newspapers, many of them on the front page. In February 1995 *Toronto Star* reporter Jack Lakey wrote:

Family members of a powerful Metro union boss with close ties to the NDP received plum jobs at the union's provincially funded housing projects, contrary to government policy.

Michael J. Reilly, business manager of Labourers' Local 183, ruled the union with blustery Irish charm and an iron will until he retired Feb. 9. As chairperson of the union's non-profit housing program, Reilly was instrumental in securing at least $44 million in provincial government loan guarantees to build two social housing developments. Reilly signed the application papers for both.

Reilly's son and two of his sons-in-law earn their livings at those buildings, and two other social housing projects operated by the union.

The story went on to detail some questionable practices and a month later Lakey followed up:

The board of directors in charge of government-funded housing operated by a big Metro union have resigned over allegations of nepotism and conflict of interest.

A *Saturday Star* story outlined how the son and son-in-law of Michael J. Reilly, former boss of Labourers' Local 183, got high-paying work with no job competition at the union's social housing projects. Local 183 runs four social housing projects built with government funds, which are overseen by a six-member non-profit property management board composed of union officials.

Joe Mancinelli, manager of the Laborer Union's central Canada office, asked for the resignations of the Local 183's executive board "We're showing that we are going to take action so things are done properly," said Mancinelli, who took over supervision of day-to-day operations at Local 183.

CHAPTER 37

ON NEGOTIATION

An entire book would not be adequate to describe the many strategies and principles in the negotiating process. I will limit myself to describing the most common principles I used during the numerous negotiations I conducted over the years.

Let me start by saying that negotiating is not a science but an art: the art of compromise. One can even say the art of life. We negotiate consciously or unconsciously all the time with ourselves, within our families, in the workplace. In fact, we negotiate almost everywhere we go and in everything we do. We decide what to eat and when to eat but we compromise over what we like and what is healthy. Without compromises a marriage would not last.

Labour negotiations are a class by themselves. In my experience, both sides should take the constructive approach and be guided by the principle that we must live with each other, just as in a marriage, and attempt to find accommodations which give something to both.

At the end of a negotiating process there should not be any clear winner or loser. The best result is when both sides are equally dissatisfied. One may think he gave too much, the other that he should have got more. Two negatives make a positive.

If one party gets a clear victory over the other, it will be only a matter of time before the losing party attempts to get even. It creates an atmosphere of mistrust and sets the stage for "getting even" or revenge.

This unreasonableness can happen on both sides. There are employers who could easily offer reasonable increases but will instead push the union to accept cuts for the sake of higher profits. Unions in a monopoly position—those in public service, for example—may squeeze the employer to get fat settlements with higher wages or higher benefits or both but it will only be a matter of time before redress is sought. This is a key issue in public service negotiations because after the settlement it is the taxpayers who ultimately pay and they, in turn, will push politicians for redress, even if it means drastic action. Look at what happened to Detroit, Michigan, around the year 2000. The entire city structure collapsed.

I never went for the jugular even if I was in a position to do so. I had two guiding principles: the short term and the long term. For the short term what was important was the minimum our members would accept and be satisfied with. For the long term, I always looked at the impact of the wage increases on future employment.

In the private sector, employers are in business for one simple reason: to make money. Many of them are truly ingenious in finding new ways to produce more for less. If the cost of labour becomes too high, sooner or later they will find ways to do more with fewer employees. The union's responsibility to its members is to find a fair balance, something easier said than done.

Take, for instance, the residential concrete forming industry. There are many ways to construct a building superstructure: by concrete forming, steel structure, masonry, precast, and so on. A builder chooses the most economical technique, which, in

Toronto, is the concrete forming superstructure. If this building system becomes uneconomical, thousands of construction workers in the Toronto area will find their work substituted by another system.

I also learned that two sets of negotiations are never the same, just as in a game of chess. There are always variables such as the economic conditions, the personalities, the inside politics, the taste left over for each party from prior negotiations, and the question of whether or not leadership is facing an election.

Visualization is an important tool. Before any set of negotiations, I would attempt to visualize the situation, almost in a military style. I would analyze the opposition's position, their strengths, their weaknesses, their possible moves, and how I might break through their defences. I would use the same process for our own position, trying to visualize the negotiation from their perspective. Sometimes I would march up and down my basement to the sound of military music until the whole scheme became clear to me.

It is critically important to scrutinize everything realistically, neither overestimating nor underestimating either side's position. I would always keep the high ground, not conceding anything, until I was fairly satisfied that the other side would meet me at the desired point.

Fair play, trust, and bargaining in good faith are the pillars of progress. If one is trusted to keep his word and if there is no perception of malice, the stage is set to obtain a fair settlement. Of course, these are not qualities easy to achieve because trust is built up over a long period of time and tested often along the way.

Flexibility in the negotiating process is a must. I usually had a master plan but it was used as a framework. Unexpected developments and roadblocks would make it necessary to modify both strategy and tactics, something you cannot do if you take a rigid approach from the outset. Sometimes, unfortunately, one has to lower expectations.

As I have mentioned a number of times in my story, off-the-record bargaining can be crucial to a peaceful settlement. It allows both parties to completely trust each other and to open up to each other.

It takes two to tango, the saying goes, yet as in dancing someone has to lead a negotiation and a good negotiator also has to be a good leader. He must have the intestinal fortitude to tell his people not what they like to hear but the reality of their situation, even if it may be unpleasant. He must sometimes be blunt, always truthful, and possess a good balance between the art of compromise, and leadership.

Over the years I gained a lot of experience from renewing collective agreements and here is what I learned. First and foremost, consult the members, give them an opportunity to voice their aspirations, usually at a special meeting. And when they do speak, you must listen.

I chose or elected the most militant and outspoken members for my negotiating committees, for the simple reason that if I was able to convince them, the rest of the membership would follow.

Most members have no idea of how the negotiating process works. They believe the union should ask for what they believe they are entitled to and that the employer should give it. That is not reality, of course. Only when members participate in the negotiating process do they realize the difficulties.

Having a militant committee is also useful for dealing with employers. Quite often employers believe union proposals are really union demands that do not reflect the attitudes of employees who they suppose to be happy. When confronted with a negotiating committee of militant working members, this perception changes.

The initial bargaining meetings are a ritual, almost like a Mexican hat dance. Both parties try to feel out and test each other. Each side tries to maintain the high ground. There are many speeches from both sides, sometimes almost sermons, to underscore the sanctity of each position or proposal, although in many cases they are mostly designed to impress their own side.

The real negotiations take place in another arena, the off-the-record one, either on the golf course, or over a lunch or a cup of coffee. It may sound easy but it is difficult.

An employer will never open up unless he has the complete trust of the person on the other side. This can only be achieved through a reputation of character built over a long period of time. Only if each party is truly assured that the conversation will remain off the record, completely confidential, will the discussion be truly open and honest.

Sometimes the real differences are so strong that even this process may not bring a satisfactory compromise. For me, however, it worked most of the time and thus avoided unnecessary strikes.

Speaking of which, not all strikes should be avoided. It becomes necessary, sometimes, to have a therapeutic strike. Members often believe any peaceful settlement could have been improved by using the strike weapon. If there are continuous fair settlements as the result of honest and skilful negotiations, it can create doubts in members' minds and suspicions of sweetheart deals between management and union leadership.

In a few cases (fortunately, very few), I thought it was better to negotiate a settlement through a strike than reach the same settlement by smart negotiation. The members saw those settlements as "their victory" rather than as due to my skill as a negotiator.

Homework is critical. I took advantage at every opportunity I had to talk to individual members or small groups to learn their bottom lines. I did this in an indirect way to hide my true intentions. I would do the same with individual employers.

Planning is also critical. If a strike ever became a strong possibility, I would speed up or slow down the negotiating process to coincide with the most opportune time to strike.

I always ensured that I did not get too close to a settlement line unless I was reasonably sure it was there. It is easier to negotiate the first dollar than the last quarter.

The voting process for the ratification is also a critical element. Not only must it be done right but it must be seen to be done right. Before taking any vote, I would open the ballot boxes, show the members that they were empty, and assign the negotiating committee or other members to carry out the vote and count the ballots. I never got involved or assigned full-time union representatives to this process, eliminating any doubt that the vote was rigged.

Finally, I cannot emphasize enough the importance of common sense and fair compromise. One must always keep in mind that we have to live with the opposition. They are the ones providing the jobs.

Those were my guidelines. If one considers my thirty-two years of union activities, I daresay I have acquired considerable experience. My big takeaway is that if the members trust their leader, it is always easier for them to accept a settlement. Often I was told by members that they voted in favour "because you told us this is the best we can do and we trust you."

I was fortunate in 1963 to attend the seven-week course sponsored by the Canadian Labour Congress's Labour College in Montreal, and in 1974 the Trade Union Program at Harvard University. I think that I am the only Canadian trade unionist who attended both of those programs. Those courses helped me better service our membership and promote their cause. I feel sorry for newly elected or appointed union representatives who go from the work site or assembly line to a union administration position. They may be intelligent, well spoken, and even well educated but they have little or no knowledge of the union's many administrative operations and these are important to members. While some big unions such as the United Steelworkers of America and UNIFOR have instituted good training programs for newly hired staff, most smaller unions and construction unions do not have anything like that available. New leaders learn through the school of hard knocks. There should be a better way to prepare them. I would urge institutions of higher learning to institute a semester or more of union administration courses, teaching labour law, basic accounting (including the importance of financial statements), various aspects of government programs such as Unemployment Insurance and Workers Compensation, pension fund structures, the grievance procedure, arbitration, basic negotiations, safety laws, and trust fund administration.

Economics is important. It is surprising how very few people have an understanding of monetary and fiscal policy, government budgets, government debts and deficits, and their effect on the economy. All these things ultimately drive jobs. The more informed and educated our union representatives, the greater asset they will be to a union and to society, because, to paraphrase a famous writer: no union is an island.

Perhaps most crucially, labour leaders of the future need to understand what happened before them. They need to appreciate the challenges overcome by previous generations of workers and the hard-won rights negotiated by their many dedicated predecessors in union leadership roles. They need to learn labour history for, as William Faulkner famously wrote in *Requiem for a Nun*, "The past is never dead. It's not even past."

ACKNOWLEDGEMENTS

I would like to thank Ian Harvey for organizing the initial draft of this manuscript, doing the additional research to find historical facts and dates to augment my memories, and working with me to create the finished product.